It's Your Money

ACHIEVING FINANCIAL
WELL-BEING

A Guide and Journal

KAREN McCALL

"Whatever you can do or dream you can, begin it.
Boldness has genius, power, and magic in it."
—Goethe

CHRONICLE BOOKS

San Francisco

Design By Levin Breidenbach Wade
Manufactured in China
Typeset in Sabon MT, Trade Gothic, Trixie, and Zapf Dingbats

Library of Congress Cataloging-in-Publication Data:
McCall, Karen.
It's Your Money: Achieving Financial Well-Being: A Guide and Journal.
p. cm.
ISBN 0-8118-2503-5 (hc)
1. Finance, Personal.   2. Money.   I. Title.
HG179 .M237 2000
332.024'01—dc21   99-087436

Distributed in Canada by
Raincoast Books
9050 Shaughnessy Street
Vancouver, B.C. V6P 6E5

10 9 8 7 6 5 4 3 2 1

Chronicle Books LLC
85 Second Street
San Francisco, CA 94105
www.chroniclebooks.com

This book is dedicated to my clients,
who have been—and continue to be—
my greatest teachers, and whose lives
bear profound witness to what can happen
when we face our fears and take control of our financial lives.

Thirteen years ago, I opened the doors to my business, Financial Recovery. My goal was to help people create a new relationship to money—to shed their self-defeating money behaviors and build for themselves a new financial life, one characterized not by disarray and deprivation but by a sense of plenty and peace of mind.

The passion and commitment behind this new career had its roots in my own experience: my own financial life had been a jumble some years before I began my new business. Of course, I thought this was a well-kept secret; on the outside I looked every inch the part of a successful young professional woman. And like my colleagues, I had had tremendous financial opportunities presented to me by the company I worked for. But unlike my friends and coworkers, I was tossing security away. My firm had a very generous ESOP (Employee Stock Ownership Program), for example. But instead of holding onto my shares, I was constantly selling them—not always at the best price—and using the money to live on.

Some years before this I had received a substantial amount of money from a divorce settlement. I quickly stashed it in a savings account at my bank and thought no more about it. Savings were good, weren't they? And after all, my money was earning a little interest. One day my uncle invited me to confide in him by asking me eagerly, "Did you put the money in a mutual fund?" I was too embarrassed to ask what a mutual fund was. I could tell he thought it would be a good idea. I wanted his approval, so I answered simply, "Yes."

The truth was that I had no idea what a mutual fund, or an IRA, or any other kind of investment was. I'd just never been exposed to those terms. But I was too proud to admit that I didn't know what my uncle was talking about, and I was too ashamed to ask him or anyone else for help. Those years in my life were filled with chaos and confusion, and I was consumed by fear of the financial jeopardy in which I was living.

I knew there was more at work than my lack of understanding of financial matters; I knew there were emotional issues that undermined my success with money. So I started searching for help. I looked for books on the subject but found few on the shelves. I sought out therapists, but either the suffering I was experiencing wasn't taken seriously, or they simply didn't know how to help.

I knew the only hope for me was to find a way of integrating the practical, emotional, and spiritual aspects of my relationship to money. It was my acceptance of this responsibility–the realization that no one else would or could do the job for me–that allowed me to begin building a new kind of financial life for myself.

BRIDGING THE GAP

I wasn't sure that my new business would succeed. What I did know, however, was that the financial recovery process, which had evolved from my personal experiences, worked. As it turned out, my fears about striking out on my own were unfounded. The new business was successful from the start. I'm convinced that one of the reasons is that I was not simply serving as a guide but had taken the journey myself.

I think a more important reason that my practice grew as quickly as it did, though, is that it filled a critical need. When I started my business, there were budget counselors and consumer credit advisors on the one hand, and financial planners and accountants on the other. There was nothing in between. For those who struggled with their relationship to money, as I once had, there were few options. The financial recovery process was profoundly effective at bridging that gap, especially for people for whom nothing else had worked.

As my clients moved through the stages of the financial recovery process, examining some of the underlying issues that had shaped their relationship to money and developing sound financial behaviors, the time would come when I'd feel they were ready to move from looking at current financial needs to planning for a financial future. It was at about this point that I would start to see on their faces the same expressions that must have played across my own when my uncle asked me about mutual funds. I'd watch as they stiffened in their seats and their eyes glazed over when we talked about doing a will, opening an IRA, or pricing term life insurance. They would come back for our next meeting having taken none of the action steps we'd discussed. What should have been a time of exhilaration and celebration at how far they had come was instead an experience characterized by confusion and hesitation.

In their inability to move confidently into the process of planning their financial future–their sense of "overwhelm" at where to start, whom to trust, and what financial products to consider–my clients were, and are, not alone. It is estimated that as many as fifty million Americans have no basic health insurance. There are millions more who have no life insurance. A study by one of America's largest brokerage firms showed that the vast majority of Baby Boomers in the United States have saved less than $3,000 toward their retirement. While I was writing this book, savings as a percentage of disposable personal income had decreased to minus five percent according to the United States Bureau of Economic Analysis–and experts say that those who do save don't invest the money they have. At the most basic level, this means that vast numbers of people are at risk of being unable to withstand a serious illness, a natural disaster, or a major economic recession. Looking ahead a decade or two, it also means that there are many, many men and women who, as they grow older, will have lifestyles that are radically different from the ones they enjoy today, in many cases simply because they did not know how to begin.

If you have tried many times to save money, only to see it drained away by an emergency or other unplanned spending; if you have spent years thinking about planning for retirement or investing your money but procrastinated again and again, waiting for the day when you have "just a little more cash"; if you, like so many of my clients, are caught in the gap between where you are and where you want to go, this book is for you.

how to **Use** this book

I didn't want this to be strictly a "how-to" book on financial planning. There are many such books already on the market and there is a wealth of information and resources available on the Internet. Nor is this designed to make you an expert on the various investment products one sees advertised at every turn. Instead, I've based this guide on the principles of the financial recovery process that have come from the work my clients and I do together, because no matter what one's background is, no matter what one's goals are, it is a process that works. My thirteen years of experience as a financial counselor have confirmed for me again and again that even people who have never saved or invested before can change the course of their financial lives by starting with the basics.

I'm going to show you how to get in touch with some of the obstacles that have been holding you back and how to gain the knowledge that will help you move forward with your financial life. We'll also be establishing what steps you need to take to put together a solid foundation for your personal financial planning. Once you have gained clarity about your obstacles and learned some tools for building around them, I'm betting that you'll begin to feel a sense of excitement about the possibilities that lie ahead. So we'll also spend time talking about the importance of including financial professionals in your financial life, and we'll talk about getting you ready to develop and implement a financial plan for your life.

As you work through the pages of this journal, you will learn:

* How to assess your current money behaviors and what they're really costing you

* How to build a realistic plan for spending

* The importance of assessing your belief systems and attitudes about money

* What behavioral changes you may want to make in order to stabilize your financial life

* Why gaining knowledge about the principles of personal finance is key to creating a strong financial structure

* How to identify your short- and long-term needs

* How to assemble the layers of your financial life in a way that provides a solid foundation for successfully planning your future

You're going to be creating a Monthly Spending Plan. You'll also develop a more comprehensive Annual Spending Plan that will help you clarify—and achieve—your vision of the life you want to have. You'll find a number of exercises that call for you to put pen to paper. When you come to one of these, take your time. Be thoughtful about your answers. The writing process has a way of surprising us with what it reveals. The questions on these pages are designed to help you assess your financial life in a way that connects your head and your heart.

I also want to encourage you to use the spaces provided throughout this book not only to write down ideas but to start expressing your thoughts and feelings about money and your relationship to it. This will be an essential piece of the work if you truly want to reinvent your financial behavior and create a sound future.

THE IMPORTANCE OF "BEGINNER'S MIND"

You're about to embark on an intense process, and you may feel a little overwhelmed: How do I start? Is it too late for me? How do I sort out a dizzying assortment of ideas and information? Dare I hope for a better future?

I encourage my clients and students to approach the process with what the Eastern philosophers call "beginner's mind." Several years ago, when my oldest grandson, Mathieu, was in kindergarten, he came home one day and announced proudly to my daughter Terri that he had been named "Student of the Week." Terri praised him effusively and off he went, smiling. A few minutes later, he was back. "Mommy," he asked in a soft voice, "what's a student?" In the way of the very young, Mathieu had not been at all afraid to ask such a basic question.

Whenever we're approaching something new, it serves us well to reclaim the innocence with which we're all born–that state of mind that allows us to be unashamedly curious about the simple things; vitally interested in seeing all that is new; and deeply, profoundly teachable.

WHY NOT YOU?

The late psychologist Abraham Maslow is said to have asked one of his classes: "Which of you believe that you will achieve greatness?" The class stared back at him, no one answering. Maslow said quietly, "If not you, who then?"

When it comes to financial planning, why not you? And why not now? When I ask my clients why they have put off financial planning, the most frequent answers I get in return are, "Well, because I'm too old." "Because I'm too young; I have plenty of time." "Because I don't know anything about investing." "Because I don't have enough money yet." Statistics tell us that procrastination is the number one reason people fail financially. If you're putting off planning your financial future because you're scared, because you don't know what to do first, or because you don't know whom to trust, remember that the two keys to getting started are "You" and "Now."

If you start today, you can create a more solid financial future, no matter what your age or situation is. A good example of what can happen when you set fear aside and start taking action is the case of Louise, a woman who first came to see me several years ago, when she was sixty-three years old. In Louise's case, it did seem too late, and she was immobilized by fear. When we first met, Louise told me that she was "underemployed and under-earning" and had used up most of her money. Several years before, she had been through a divorce that gave her a sizable settlement. Following the divorce, Louise–at that time a psychotherapist in private practice– cut her business in half by closing one of her two offices. Then she decided to switch careers and try to build a new practice as a personal development coach.

By the time Louise came to see me, not only had she run through the money she'd received from her divorce, but she was unable to keep making the payments on the large balances she'd run up on her credit cards. She was scared, and she told me, "I never thought I'd be old and poor." But as Louise got some basics in place she began to achieve results beyond anything she could have imagined when she first began the process. Today she is completely out of debt. She's increased her earnings from $31,000 a year to $160,000 a year. She recently funded a pension plan for an initial $40,000, and this year paid her income taxes on time. Freed from the burden of debt and the fear of what will happen to her as she grows older, Louise has begun to blossom, using her energy and creativity for the benefit of both her clients and herself. She also realizes that she must continue to move her financial life forward: if not she, who; if not now, never.

MY WISH FOR YOU

Once, after I had finished teaching a class on how to prepare for successful financial planning, a woman came up to me at the end of the final session just bursting with enthusiasm. She'd been very cautious and fearful about money in general when she'd started the class, without a clue about financial planning. I will never forget the look in her eyes as she said to me, "I can't wait to get started!" I'm hopeful that you will come away from these pages energized by new ideas and with a plan of action for building your financial future. It's also my hope that you'll gain a deeper understanding of the underlying feelings that have, until now, prevented you from using your money in ways that serve you well.

The
Financial
Hierarchy

**Because you have picked up this book, chances are you feel your finan-
cial life lacks direction or structure. But the truth is that although you
may not recognize it or like the way it looks, you do have a financial
structure to your life. I'm betting, though, that whether it's a feeling of
instability, chronic unmanageability, or simply a lack of knowledge, there
is at least one way you feel your current approach isn't working for you.**

THE MONEY/LIFE DRAIN

I see examples of unstable financial structures all the time. They are
characterized not only by the burden of debt or by shaky financial
practices but also by signs of a predictable—and progressive—downward slide. I call it the "Money/Life Drain." Signs that you're
caught in this downward spiral include a lifestyle where the
demands on your time, energy, and money leave nothing for the
things that make life worth living. When you are unable to save and
are pressured to work more and earn more, your relationships
become strained, your health is impacted by the stress, and ulti-
mately your overall quality of life deteriorates. You are filled with
despair and hopelessness.

   Does this seem extreme? Believe me, it's not. I see people from
all walks of life—women and men in all lines of work, even people
with inherited wealth—and all have similar descriptions of an existence that leaves them stripped of their life force as they struggle to
make ends meet. A report issued by the U.S. Census Bureau in 1999
found that even the well-off were living dangerously close to financial instability. The survey reported that eight million Americans
whose families earned more than $45,000 a year said they still had
trouble paying for rent, medical bills, and other basic daily needs.
Twenty percent of Americans nationwide reported problems paying
essential bills. There are millions of women and men who don't
think of themselves as living close to the financial edge until a
large, unexpected expense—or sometimes even a small one—puts
them over the line. As one woman said, "I think a lot of people out
there think they're getting by and doing fine and don't realize how
devastating it can be."

The Money/Life Drain

FINANCIAL BURDENS, DEBT, OUT-OF-CONTROL EXPENSES

INABILITY TO SAVE; PRESSURE TO
EARN/WORK MORE

RELATIONSHIPS STRESSED

HEALTH AND WELL-BEING
COMPROMISED

FINANCIAL,
EMOTIONAL,
AND
SPIRITUAL
DEPLETION

The Money/Life Drain illustrates how an undependable financial structure, top-heavy and weak, can erode the very things that make life worth living. As spiraling consumer debt and an inability to save shove us into a cycle of "work more to earn more," we lose sight of the fact that work, as writer Studs Terkel put it in his book *Working,* should be "about a search...for daily meaning as well as daily bread."

In their book *Your Money or Your Life,* Vicki Robin and the late Joe Dominguez observe that "over time our relationship with money—earning it, spending it, investing it, owing it, protecting it, worrying about it—has taken over the major part of our lives." Robin and Dominguez cite studies showing that as many as 90 percent of all divorces are caused by conflicts about money, and a survey in which 48 percent of 4,126 male executives interviewed saw their lives as "empty and meaningless" despite years of professional striving. In his book *The Roaring 2,000s,* economic forecaster and business consultant Harry Dent observes, "Surveys of happiness in this country have shown that wealth affects the sense of well-being by a factor of only 2 percent. Happiness," he goes on, "is more about relationships, friends, family...community...and a balanced life."

We won the revolution—the Industrial Revolution, which promised a higher standard of living for all—but lost the war. We adopted a new way of life that called for us to "push for a higher standard of living regardless of moral, ethical, emotional, cultural, marital, environmental, and political consequences."

Are there any parts of your life that you feel have been compromised by your behaviors and beliefs around money? How have those parts of your life been affected? How does this feel?

The Financial Hierarchy

The Financial Hierarchy

What you may be experiencing is the weight of an unsupported—and unsupportable—financial structure. To change these feelings you need to change the shaky financial structure.

BUILDING A NEW KIND OF FINANCIAL STRUCTURE

The more experience I gained as a counselor and the more I watched my clients' processes as they began building (or rebuilding) sound financial lives, the more I was reminded of what the late psychologist Abraham Maslow called the "hierarchy of human needs." Just as his pyramidal structure for a sound emotional life depended on first having met one's basic human needs, I began to see that a healthy financial life rests upon a foundation of having met certain fundamental financial needs.

I say "certain fundamental financial needs," but the truth is, clients come to me to discuss more than the state of their financial lives (though many think that's the single reason they are there). It's not just about how we handle money but also about our lifestyle, and the ways our financial choices affect every part of our lives long after the spending decisions are made. I observed that as people began establishing a solid foundation they started to discover ways around their financial obstacles—paths that were very different from simply working harder. Their ways of spending and handling money changed. The clarity they gained helped increase their feelings of self-esteem, which, in turn, allowed them to begin looking at providing for more than just their simplest needs. It was at this point that they began assessing their safety and security needs (insurance and savings, for example), educating themselves, and developing a plan of action.

As feelings of self-worth and competence continued to increase, clients also began experiencing—often for the first time in their lives—a freedom from fear. They found that for the first time they had the clarity, and the courage, to acknowledge that the way they dealt with their financial life had affected the quality of their entire life. This led them to undertake a realistic assessment of their own value system.

The Financial Hierarchy Pyramid

Behaviors

Reaching your full potential; becoming all you can be

Examining money behaviors in your personal and professional relationships

Clarifying values about spending, saving, earning; Annual Spending Plan; finding money to begin investing

Assessing your savings, insurance, etc.; identifying what knowledge you need to gain; developing action steps

Tracking income and expenses; creating a Monthly Spending Plan; exploring belief systems around money (and their obstacles); debt management

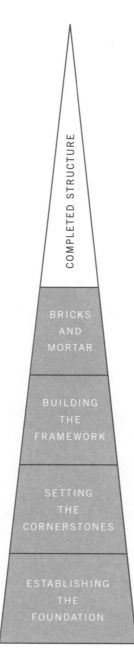

COMPLETED STRUCTURE

BRICKS AND MORTAR

BUILDING THE FRAMEWORK

SETTING THE CORNERSTONES

ESTABLISHING THE FOUNDATION

Benefits

Peace of mind and financial well-being

More genuine relationships with others

Understanding behaviors that support the foundation; continued increase in self-esteem; the beginning of hope

Clarity and understanding of your safety and protection needs; increased feelings of self-esteem; the beginning of freedom from fear

Clarity and understanding of spending and debt; learning to live within your means; building around obstacles that have kept you from reaching your financial (and other) goals

With new understanding and the beginning of hope, clients turned naturally to examining their money behaviors in relation to others—an effort that would lead, in time, to more genuine relationships with the people in their lives. It was at this point that I would see people begin to bloom, to bring their dreams and aspirations to life at last. I call this path of interrelated tasks and profound changes the Financial Hierarchy.

I'd like you to think of constructing a new financial structure for yourself—your personal "financial pyramid." You're going to build one layer at a time, taking on the developmental tasks described for each level. Focusing on one layer at a time will make the job of overhauling your financial life much less intimidating and a lot more manageable. Dividing the work into smaller pieces will also help ensure that you'll have the time and energy to savor the profound internal meaning of the changes you are making. Best of all, when you're through you'll have a strong edifice—one that's built on a solid foundation, using good materials, and with no shortcuts having been taken.

Just because you don't have one level perfected doesn't mean you can't go to work on another level. For example, if you are a parent and have no life insurance, that's not something you want to put off any longer; so while you might still be building the foundation of your new financial structure, it makes perfect sense to also be assessing some of your safety and security needs, like insurance, which are part of Level Two. Just remember that a failure to address the basic elements first will eventually affect the overall integrity of the structure you're attempting to build.

The 5

Levels of the
Financial
Hierarchy

Over the years, I've had the thrill of seeing clients modify their financial behaviors time and again, building and sustaining lives that are more rewarding not only financially, but in every other way. I want the same for you. You're going to use the principles behind the Financial Hierarchy to begin planning your way toward peace of mind. Each level of the Financial Hierarchy is an invitation to assess where you are financially and to explore the emotional components of your financial situation and your relationship to money.

LEVEL ONE: LAYING THE FOUNDATION

To know where you are going, you must first know where you are. So your first task is to put some financial basics into place—bottom-line practices that form the foundation of any sound financial life. These include:

* Managing your checkbook effectively

* Tracking expenses and income

* Creating a Monthly Spending Plan

* Developing a plan for debt management/reduction

* Examining your money history and the emotional components that contribute to your behaviors with money

The result of this careful dealing with financial basics is that you will begin to gain a sense of clarity about your financial picture. It is always empowering for people when they reach this point. Sometimes the truth really does set us free!

LEVEL TWO: SETTING THE CORNERSTONES

Once you've gained some clarity about your money history and behaviors and learned some tools for living within your means and managing debt, you'll set the cornerstones of your new financial life by:

* Assessing your savings

* Assessing your insurance (what you have and what you may need)

* Closing the gaps in your knowledge

* Developing a plan of action

Now you will begin to feel a growing sense of competence as you begin taking responsibility for your financial life. Your sense of self-esteem will also begin to grow, along with new feelings of safety and security.

LEVEL THREE: BUILDING THE FRAMEWORK

The long-standing attitudes and beliefs we hold about money play a key role in shaping the values by which we live our lives. But if the system from which they grew was distorted, then our values will also be mis-shapen. This is the stage at which you really need to begin coming to terms with your financial behaviors so that you can begin making different choices. Your tasks at this stage are:

* Developing an Annual Spending Plan

* Clarifying values

* Coming to terms with what isn't working

* Finding money to begin investing

By this stage your new financial structure is really beginning to take shape. You are making decisions based on knowledge of your financial reality, bolstered by a fuller understanding of where your behaviors related to money came from and how they have been affecting your financial choices. As you learn to work around the obstacles that formerly blocked your way, you will begin to experience a sense of hope and exhilaration.

LEVEL FOUR: BRICKS AND MORTAR

Now the structure of your new financial life is really coming together. But if it is to stand up to the passing years, and to the various forces that will assail it, it will need to be reinforced at every key point. This stage and its tasks are the "bricks and mortar" that will make your financial life strong as you begin:

* Examining how your relationship to money affects the people in your life

* Looking at the ways those around you can impact your financial life

* Considering the role financial professionals can play in helping you build a strong financial life

As you complete this stage, you will begin to reap the rewards that good money management practices can provide. You will see how your financial behaviors can impact those around you in a positive way. With the order and stability you've developed in the first few levels of your new financial life—and with a lighter heart—you are able to focus on the true fundamentals of life: living, learning, and growing as a human being. You feel an increasing sense of purpose.

With your true needs met through the sturdy structure you've created, your financial, emotional, and spiritual energy can be put to work in new and more rewarding ways. Now you have a genuine opportunity to:

*   Continue to increase your financial wealth and overall sense of well-being

*   Experience the joy and satisfaction of realizing your dreams and goals

*   Enjoy true peace of mind

This is it—what makes the hard work worthwhile. With your financial structure built on a solid foundation—and, with regular maintenance, made to last—you are free to live out your life's potential. This is the ultimate wealth.

32

The Five Levels of Financial Hierarchy

Level

1

Laying the

Foundation

In Level One of the financial pyramid, you're dealing with some pretty basic elements of your financial life. I don't mean to assume that because you're reading this book you don't have any of these pieces in place. You may be doing some, or even all, of the Level One tasks now. But it's important for you to assess whether what you have been doing works for you and isn't hampering your ability to meet your bigger financial goals.

In Level One you will learn:

*   The importance of managing your checkbook

*   How to begin tracking your expenses and
    your income

*   How to create a Monthly Spending Plan

*   How to develop a realistic debt repayment plan

*   About the emotional components of your money behaviors
    as you write your Money Autobiography

MANAGING YOUR CHECKBOOK EFFECTIVELY

How would you feel if anyone else saw the inside of your checkbook register? You may be someone whose checkbook maintenance is flawless, but some people have an adverse reaction at the mere thought of analyzing a checkbook. It's important to get honest about the shape your checkbook is in and take steps to clean it up if needed.

Do you keep a running balance in your checkbook? One woman I knew thought of her checkbook habits as impeccable. "I write everything down," she would assert. It was true that she wrote down the amount of every check. But her checkbook register always had a lot of white space where things like check numbers, dates, and ATM transactions should have been.

Do you bounce checks or rely on overdraft protection to "pick up the slack"? What are the fees each time you do? As I'm sure you know, banks are happy when you utilize their overdraft protection services: it makes money for them. One of my clients came in one day to report that she had been $.50 short in her checking account that week, and it had cost her $50.00 in fees!

Do you enter ATM transactions regularly, or do the slips get lost and force you to "guesstimate" what you withdrew? My friend's mother, a confirmed "guesstimator," regularly had discrepancies of hundreds of dollars between the balance she thought was in her checking account and what was actually there. She dealt with this by penciling in a second column along the edge of her check register, running two totals each month: "Bank Says" and "I Say."

Get out your bank statements for the last six months and make a list of all the fees associated with:

Bounced checks:

The use of overdraft protection:

ATM transaction fees:

What was the total for all these activities?

List three more-rewarding ways in which you could have spent
this money:

1

2

3

Whether the way you handle your checkbook is or isn't working well for you, I strongly suggest that you record all the activity in your checkbook by hand for a while. If you're one of the millions of people who use a computer software program to help you keep your checkbook straight, you may feel as if I'm asking you to revert to the Stone Age and scratch your numbers in the dust. Managing a checkbook electronically certainly works for some people. But at a meeting of financial counselors I attended recently, we all concurred that we'd rarely seen a client with a "computerized" checkbook register who could give a completely accurate rundown of exactly what was in his or her checking account. Truly evaluating how you manage your checking account, when combined with tracking your daily expenses, gives you clarity about your finances and connects you to your money behaviors.

TRACKING EXPENSES AND INCOME

Another essential part of becoming clear about your finances is to learn to track where your money is going. This involves writing down everything you spend and earn. Most people know that they should track their spending, but few actually do it. "Too time-consuming, too tedious, and besides, only people with 'money problems' have to track their expenses," clients will often protest. In fact, the opposite is true. People who never seem to worry about money—from the very wealthy to those who simply seem to be in control financially—track their spending very carefully.

HERE'S HOW IT WORKS

How many times have you gone to an ATM machine and withdrawn $20—or $200—only to wonder the next day where all of it went? The "black hole" into which cash falls is a big issue for most people. You should keep track of your cash spending in exactly the same way you keep track of the money that comes out of your checking account. You want the same results: an accurate picture at any given time of how much money you have available to you.

Use two check registers, one for checks, and one for writing down every single cash expenditure you make. Here's how:

1. Take an empty checkbook register and write on the first line the amount of cash you currently have on hand.

2. Whenever you spend cash, note on the next line what it was for, and then subtract the amount from the original cash-on-hand entry you made, just as you would record a check in your checkbook.

3. If you receive any cash, enter this in your cash register as a "deposit," noting where it came from. Add this to your most recent cash-on-hand total.

4. At the end of the day, count up your cash. The amount you have should match the amount showing on the last line in your cash register.

THE HIGH COST OF "IMPULSE" BUYS

After you've been tracking your expenses for a while, you'll probably be in for some surprises. I'll bet you didn't know how much those morning lattes were adding up to week after week. Tracking your expenses will help you identify the small expenditures that can add up to big money over the course of a year. Using the information you get from tracking your cash expenditures, you can evaluate what effect those expenditures are having on your overall financial condition and whether or not you could be using that money in more meaningful ways.

Later on, you'll be creating a list of your own most common impulse buys. I'll ask you to evaluate whether or not they're worth the cost, financial or otherwise. The point is that tracking your money helps you build awareness about your spending choices. Most people find that after they've been doing this kind of tracking for a while, they spend less. One of my students once told me, "I wanted to buy it, but the thought of having to write it down stopped me." If it's not worth writing down, it's probably not worth buying. It's been said that you may not make your first million by tracking your spending and keeping your checkbook up to date, but you won't keep your first million without tracking where your money is going and maintaining your checkbook.

Impulse-Spending Chart

	WEEKLY COSTS FOR COMMON IMPULSE BUYS	ANNUAL COST
Paperback book	$ 8.50	$ 442
Tulips	7.00	364
Caffe lattes (twice a week)	5.00	260
Greeting cards	6.00	312
Snacks	10.00	520
Total	$ 36.50	$ 1,898

Interest on charged items: $303

Extra money available if you curb impulse spending: $2,201

Do any of your weekly impulse purchases change the quality of your life? I don't mean to imply that you'll never want to spend money on a book, greeting card, or flowers. But are you buying things you don't need? Cards you never send? If the answer is yes, then you might want to take a closer look at this kind of spending. Curbing your impulse spending can give you significant additional cash for saving or investing.

Along with managing your checkbook and tracking income and expenses, there's another important building block you want to have in your financial foundation: a Monthly Spending Plan. This is simply a blueprint for daily spending that gives you an opportunity to see the consequences of your choices while you still have time to do something about these choices.

There are three primary stumbling blocks that can derail your efforts to get and stay on a solid financial footing:

* Spending more than you earn

* Failing to provide for your true needs

* Neglecting to evaluate the ways you use credit, what it's costing you, and how it's impacting your other financial decisions

The Monthly Spending Plan will help you begin to look at these obstacles and learn to work around them.

Besides giving you a sense of how your money will be used each month, there are other benefits to creating a spending plan. One of my clients told me that tracking her and her husband's expenses and income, by category, immediately reduced stress and opened up the communication between them. Another client said, "There's stuff you get at in a really emotional way when you use the structure of money."

But despite the benefits, people often feel an initial resistance to the very idea of a spending plan. I want to emphasize that a spending plan is not the same thing as a budget. Mikelann Valterra of Financial Clarity in Seattle—one of a growing number of financial counselors nationwide—describes it this way: Budgeting is listing all the money that gets paid out to others and then seeing if there is any "left over" for you. A spending plan, on the other hand, is a way of making sure your own needs are met along with your financial responsibilities, such as rent, utilities, car payments, etc. View your spending plan as a tool for getting what you want out of life.

HOW TO BUILD YOUR MONTHLY PLAN

Step One: Determine Your Spending Plan Categories

If you're like most people, you'll probably find that at first it's a challenge to define your spending categories in enough detail to be useful. That's the experience a client of mine had when she tried, prior to our first appointment, to come up with the various categories in which she spent money. Sheila arrived at my office her first day clutching a small slip of paper on which she'd written down Food, Housing, Transportation, and Miscellaneous. She (like almost all of my new clients) was amazed as we sat together and defined her spending categories more thoughtfully, breaking out even relatively small but specific expenditures like dry cleaning, soft drinks, and bridge tolls. We also talked about what goes where. When Sheila went grocery shopping, for example, she tended to buy many other items and supplies while she was in the store. So I reminded her that things like toiletries, magazines, flowers, and household supplies are not food, and we placed these items in more appropriate categories.

Here are some of the most common categories that you'll need in your spending plan:

Home	Clothing	Education
Food	Health Care	Savings
Self Care	Transportation	Investments
Entertainment	Vacation/Travel	Debt Repayment
Gifts	Dependent Care	Insurance
Personal Business	Taxes	

In the sample Monthly Spending Plan categories shown on pages 46-47, you'll notice that the food category has been broken down into Groceries, Breakfasts, Lunches, Dinners, Fast Food/Take-out, Coffee/Tea, Snacks/Soft Drinks, and Tips. Entertainment has been likewise divided into a number of smaller categories. As you think about your spending plan categories, it is important to work out as detailed a list as possible. You'll want to break each category down into individual subcategories that deal with specific areas of spending.

Make a list of all the categories and subcategories in which you spend money every month:

Level One

Step Two: Decide What You'll Spend

Now I'd like you to begin filling in your own Monthly Spending
Plan. Decide how much you will spend in each category this month
if you are to meet your needs. As you plug dollar amounts into your
spending plan categories, use your best estimation of what you'll
need, or want, to spend. If you've been tracking expenses and
income, you can refer to your record keeping, to past bills, and to
your checkbook to see what you've been spending and in which
categories. Check your calendar to make sure you take into account
any events, special occasions, or other activities coming up this
month that you'll want to spend money on. Later, after we've evalu-
ated whether your income can cover your planned expenses, we'll go
back and make any necessary adjustments.

Here is what two typical categories might look like in a
Monthly Spending Plan, including adjustments:

Sample Monthly Spending Plan

CATEGORY/EXPENSE	PLAN	ADJUSTMENTS	ADJUSTED PLAN
FOOD			
Groceries	$ 450	$ -35	$ 415
Breakfasts	40	-5	35
Lunches	110	-25	85
Dinners	150	-35	115
Fast Food/Take-out	25	-5	20
Coffee/Tea	35	-10	25
Snacks/Soft Drinks	20	-10	10
Tips	50	-10	40
TOTAL FOOD	880	-135	745

Sample Monthly Spending Plan

CATEGORY/EXPENSE	PLAN	ADJUSTMENTS	ADJUSTED PLAN
ENTERTAINMENT			
Tapes/CDs	$ 15	$	$ 15
Movies/Video Rentals	30		30
Theater/Ballet			
Concerts/Museums			
Dating	100	-25	75
Sporting Events			
Magazines/Newspapers	25	-5	20
Books/Hobbies	15		15
Camera/Film	30		30
Guests	30		30
Parties/Holidays			
Alcohol and Cigarettes	105	-10	95
TOTAL ENTERTAINMENT	350	-40	310

Level One

Your Monthly Spending Plan

CATEGORY/EXPENSE	PLAN	ADJUSTMENTS	ADJUSTED PLAN
	$	$(+/-)	$

CATEGORY/EXPENSE	PLAN	ADJUSTMENTS	ADJUSTED PLAN
	$	$(+/-)	$

Level One

CATEGORY/EXPENSE	PLAN	ADJUSTMENTS	ADJUSTED PLAN
	$	$(+/-)	$

CATEGORY/EXPENSE	PLAN	ADJUSTMENTS	ADJUSTED PLAN
	$	$(+/-)	$

Level One

CATEGORY/EXPENSE	PLAN	ADJUSTMENTS	ADJUSTED PLAN
	$	$(+/-)	$

CATEGORY/EXPENSE	PLAN	ADJUSTMENTS	ADJUSTED PLAN
	$	$ (+/-)	$

Once you have the amounts listed next to all your categories, add them together to get a total of all your expenses for this month.

Total Monthly Expenses	$	$(+/-)	$
Total Monthly Income			

Step Three: Determine the Income You Expect to Receive This Month

Once you've defined your spending categories, you will also want to write down your income. First write down how much you'll earn from your job or business. Then consider any other areas of inflow you may have (rental income, business reimbursements, or gifts, for example).

Step Four: Do the Math

Subtract your expenses from your income. At this point you may see that you're spending more this month than you'll be earning. Remember, the objective of a spending plan is to see the consequences of your financial choices while you still have time to do something about them.

Now let's do something about these choices.

Step Five: Review and Adjust Your Plan

If you subtracted your expenses and found you don't have the money this month to cover everything, you have two choices: you can either earn more or spend less.

The first thing we're going to do is figure out some ways for you to trim your expenses. There are two main issues I look at to adjust expenses:

1. Exploring Low- or No-Cost Ways of Meeting Some Needs

This can be an opportunity to tap into your creativity and find low- or no-cost ways to get some of the things you need. Two of my clients, for example, had been in the habit of going out to dinner and a movie every Friday night. They were tired at the end of a long week and felt they deserved some relaxation. But when they began tracking their expenses and developed a spending plan, they discovered that their Friday night outings had been costing them as much as $400 a month. June was excited when she called to tell me that she and Tommy had put their heads together and come up with a creative alternative: the previous Friday evening, they'd gone to the library and checked out a video, then stopped at the local deli for an inexpensive take-out feast.

Another couple wanted to give an outdoor party to celebrate the beginning of summer. They were convinced that to do it right, they'd have to buy new lawn furniture—at considerable expense, given their taste and eye for design. Instead, they too came up with a creative solution. They sent out invitations to a "BYO blanket" party, and guests were charmed by the spontaneity and informality of the gathering.

A year later, they received some money they hadn't expected. That summer they gave another party, but they didn't even think about buying the lawn furniture they'd once felt was so indispensable to their entertaining. Where once they would have whipped out their credit cards to make a purchase, they now pay cash for everything and have clear priorities about where their money goes.

2.   Discerning the Difference between a Want and a Need

A spending plan will highlight the ways you are—and aren't—taking care of yourself. Having a plan not only helps you evaluate how many of your needs are really being met; it's also an important tool for exploring what your needs really are. And while the National Council for Economic Education tells us that by grade four, a child should be able to describe the difference between needs and wants, the truth is that many people—long after fourth grade—aren't able to make this important distinction.

What they do instead is rationalize. In fact, most of us are masters when it comes to justifying our expenditures. For example, you might feel you "need" a new suit. But maybe a new blouse or shirt will make an old suit feel new. Or you may be looking at a larger purchase—you feel you "need" a new car, for example. It may be true that you do need another car. And while you might want it to be brand-new, a used car could allow you to meet your need in a way that fits your spending plan.

Wants can be deferred, but needs must be attended to first, either by finding a way to meet the need for less or by finding money elsewhere in your spending plan to cover the expense. Classifying wants as needs is one thing that will put you further into debt and keep you on the treadmill you're trying to escape. As you look through the expenses you listed in your spending plan, try to determine which are wants, and which are needs.

There will be certain things you can't take out; you have to pay your mortgage, for example, and buy groceries.

Make a list of everything on your plan that is a necessary expense. Be sure to write the cost of each item beside it:

ITEM	COST
	$

ITEM   COST

$

$

Once you've made your list, look at the items that are left on your plan. You will need to decide whether each of these is a want or a need. As you go, it can be helpful to try and think of each item as either a Could ("I could get a massage if I cut down in another category") or a Should ("I really should buy lunch for Bob—he's treated me so often").

Turn back to your plan on page 48 and make adjustments—removing items you don't need and adjusting the dollars you've allocated accordingly. As you make choices and have to let go (for now) of some of the things that feel important, you will probably experience a sense of loss. It may feel as if you'll never have enough money for the extras that make life seem good. But at least with this approach you have a chance; if you continue spending more than you're earning, your situation can only get worse.

MAKING THE DECISION TO EARN MORE MONEY

Sometimes I'll be sitting with clients going over a spending plan, and we'll have done all that we could to adjust expenses so that they have a plan in which their needs are provided for and the other expenditures are appropriate. Yet there is still a gap between what is to be spent and what is available to spend. This is when you need to consider whether or not you want to earn more money. Here's another place where you can really put your creativity to work. There are many terrific books on the subject of changing jobs or changing careers, and a wealth of information to be mined on the Internet. Many community colleges and other learning resources have career guidance classes that can also be helpful.

REVIEWING THE OUTCOME OF YOUR PLAN

Despite your best-laid plans, when you get to the end of the month you still may find that you've spent more than you earned. When people's spending plans don't work, it's usually for one of three reasons:

You didn't allocate enough dollars in a category.

You didn't really know what an item would cost (sometimes you need to do a little research), hadn't tracked your expenses long enough (you weren't sure how much you really needed in a particular category), or weren't able to accurately anticipate an expense.

Something unexpected came up.

An out-of-town relative fell seriously ill, and you had to travel unexpectedly, or you had a car repair expense that you couldn't have foreseen. Circumstances beyond your control will from time to time affect even your most carefully constructed spending plan. That's why it's so important to have savings: even a small savings account will help lend stability to your financial life. (We'll talk in more detail about savings when we get to Level Two.)

You spent impulsively without regard to whether you could afford it.

This is the most difficult area to address, because you have to make decisions that may not always feel good. It's often tempting to use a rationalization to justify buying what you want, regardless of whether it makes sense to buy it now. Let's take Milo, for example. He came in one day describing how he had "messed up" on his spending plan and that he had "had no choice" but to make some unplanned expenditures that month. When I asked him to describe the circumstances around these additional expenses, he told me he'd arrived an hour early for a date one evening, and to "kill time" he had wandered into the music store that was right next door. He had bought $36 worth of CDs. He also had spent an unplanned weekend at a popular bed-and-breakfast inn that month—he had charged lodging and meals ("I won't have to pay the $450 until next month," he assured me) because an old girlfriend called him up and said she was having a hard time and he wanted to cheer her up. And of course he "needed" a massage after this expensive weekend away, because he felt drained and stressed after consoling his friend for two days.

What I want you to remember is that as you create your Monthly Spending Plan, you are gaining clarity about what you really spend each month, and this gives you the power to make new choices if you want to.

Doing a monthly plan on your own may feel a little overwhelming, especially at first, but there are resources that can help support you and your new goals. I encourage you to visit the Financial Recovery Counseling Institute Web page at www.financialrecovery.com. If you decide that you want the ongoing help of a financial counselor, you may be able to find one in your area listed on this site. Some counselors are also available to work with you by telephone. Whether you set up your monthly plan on your own or with the help of a professional, it should be something that you sit down and do each month. Follow the basic outline and the steps that we have just reviewed, taking into account your needs and financial responsibilities for that particular month. Your plan can become an ongoing, useful guide, and later we will use it to help create your Annual Spending Plan.

Some years ago, there was a story that circulated widely through recovery and personal-growth groups. It went something like this:

A woman was walking down the street one day, when she fell into a hole. Stuck at the bottom of the hole, she ranted and raved about who the heck had put a hole in such a stupid place and how this falling-in-holes thing was always happening to her. It took her a long, long time to figure a way to get out of the hole.

The next day she was walking down the same street and saw that the hole was now covered with a board. Trying to walk across the board, she fell into the hole again. Now the list of people who put her in those situations had grown. She cursed those idiots who don't use the right kinds of boards to span holes that shouldn't be there in the first place. She was able to climb out of the hole, though, a little faster than she had the day before.

The next day as she was walking down this same street, she saw the hole and noticed that the board that had spanned the hole the day before had been replaced by a sturdier-looking wooden platform. She started across the yawning chasm, and was halfway to the other side when the platform gave way and she found herself, once again, at the bottom of the hole. It occurred to her that her habit of making the same choices but expecting different results wasn't working too well. But she got out of the hole in no time at all.

Two weeks later, on her usual walk, she came to the corner of the street where the hole was. She took a deep breath, turned to the right, and walked down a different street.

DEVELOPING A PLAN FOR DEBT MANAGEMENT/REDUCTION

Many people who use credit cards think that if they just tried, they could control their credit card spending. But most of these same people, in truth, are like the married couple who came to me panicked because they had amassed credit card debt of more than $45,000. Self-employed professionals earning $90,000 a year, they had accumulated debt from expenditures made for vacations, CDs, restaurant outings, clothes, veterinarian bills for their beloved pets, and many small expenditures that they couldn't even recall. Tom and Kate decided very wisely to stop using their credit cards under any circumstances. The next time they had a "cash crunch," they brainstormed and came up with the idea of selling some of their music collection—duplicate CDs and those they no longer listened to—to meet the unexpected need.

The result was that Tom and Kate felt great. They'd found a creative way for coming up with needed cash and had the unexpected additional benefit of ridding themselves of some of the clutter in their home. This became an important building block for Tom and Kate that led them to new ways of looking at how they met their financial needs. After this, they came up with additional creative solutions, including the way they billed their clients, that helped them keep their commitment to creating no more new debt. This was a period in which Tom and Kate learned some very important lessons.

If you've had a problem with debt in your life, the single most important thing you can do to improve your situation is to stop using credit cards. You may be one of those people who cannot charge "just a little." Discontinuing your use of credit cards will allow you to come face-to-face with the real issues: whether you're spending too much or earning too little. You can't continue living beyond your means and expect a different outcome.

Many people, especially those who find themselves repeatedly caught by the same self-defeating financial compulsions, discover support and spiritual sustenance at Debtor's Anonymous. You can find DA on the Web at www.debtorsanonymous.org.

What Is "Debt Management"?

One of the greatest obstacles to financial health is the debt load that so many people carry. The financial—not to mention physical and emotional—cost of debt is staggering. If you don't maintain an awareness of what you are doing with credit—and what credit is doing to you—the structure of your financial life is going to feel very shaky, regardless of how well you do in other areas.

Your ultimate goal is to eliminate debt in your life. But that will take time. Meanwhile, it's important to create a realistic plan for reducing your debts to a manageable load that allows you to get on with your life. You may feel that you're already doing this pretty well, but it's still important to take a fresh look at the role debt plays in your life, especially if you are using credit cards. If the balance on your credit cards increases or stays the same month after month despite the payments you make, you will never be free of debt. The only way you'll be able to reduce or eliminate debt is to remember the first rule of holes: If you're in one, stop digging.

Assessing Your Existing Debt

Let's take a minute to assess your existing debt. Go to your wallet, desk drawer, or wherever you keep your credit cards, and get them all out. Now list all your credit cards, noting the balance, interest rate, and limit on each card.

CREDIT CARD	BALANCE DUE	INTEREST	LIMIT
	$	%	$

TOTAL BALANCE DUE: $ _____   AVERAGE INTEREST: %

Level One

Now let's go a step further and analyze your credit card expenditures. Look at your credit card statements and the expenses on each and write down what you recall about how (or why) those expenses got on each card. Can you remember? Were the expenses the result of a big or special event, or just a bunch of small expenditures that you can't even recall?

CREDIT CARD PURCHASE   REASON FOR PURCHASE

EVALUATING THE CREATION OF ANY NEW DEBT

In building a solid financial foundation, it's very important to seriously evaluate the creation of any new debt. Doing this should help you to see the powerful effect debt can have on your life. Remember, no matter how solid your foundation is or how strong your framework, the cumulative effect of debt on your life can make it seem as if you've built your financial structure on quicksand. Knowing this should lead you to two conclusions:

* It's important to reduce your debt load, and

* It's important to evaluate the incursion of any new debt

Finding money in your spending plan for reducing your debt load means you will need to prioritize and adjust some of your other expenditures. Do this just as you did in Step Five when you were creating your original spending plan. Once you have found the extra money there are a couple of different ways to use it. Some people find it satisfying to spread this extra amount out over all their debts, proportionately reducing each one every month. Others like the process of targeting a particular debt with this extra money until it is paid off, then targeting the next debt, and so on until all debts are paid. Even if you are debt-free, you must still carefully evaluate the creation of any new debt, keeping in mind the true cost of debt service and the insidious effect that credit spending can have on your financial structure.

These are the basic elements of the solid financial management practices that make up the foundation of your own financial hierarchy. But there remains an important piece to examine, and that is the effect your own belief systems have on your way of life. The next section deals specifically with this.

EXAMINING YOUR BELIEF SYSTEMS

When I meet new clients for the first time, they invariably say that they've come to see me because they "want to understand money." What they really want is to understand why money isn't working in their lives.

There are probably a number of attitudes, anxieties, and money myths that you developed early on in life that helped shape your relationship to money. The resulting belief system may continue to drive your behavior with money today, affecting your relationships with your spouse, your children, and your friends.

For example, you may realize that you weren't taught anything about money growing up. In many families, money, like sex, is a taboo subject, and one is expected to "just naturally know" what one is expected to do. Unfortunately, from what I have seen, money behaviors seem to be learned, not genetic. Or maybe you actually did learn a lot about money early in your life but still don't seem able to achieve the financial outcomes you want. I will often be working with people on their finances and this pattern will be revealed. What we usually discover is the existence of hidden beliefs or feelings about money. These hidden beliefs and feelings become obstacles that must be explored.

WRITING A MONEY HISTORY

The financial state in which we find ourselves is not only the result of how much money we have (or don't have). The ways in which we use money also have their roots in attitudes and belief systems learned in childhood. That's why it's so important to explore the attitudes and beliefs that can keep us from reaching our financial goals.

Mary, for example, grew up as the only daughter of a single mother who had her own business. Mary's mother was very successful, working long hours six days a week to make sure her business continued to thrive. From the time Mary was quite young, her mother would give Mary her credit card on Saturdays and drive her to the mall, where Mary would spend the day shopping for new clothes. Sundays she and her mother spent the day "bonding" by going through all of Mary's new clothes. As an adult, Mary told me that she had always been baffled by her compulsive spending patterns. The behavior had become so serious that her fiancé had broken off their engagement because of Mary's habit of overspending. By connecting to the underlying emotional components of her behavior, Mary was finally able to get rid of her helplessness in the face of this very destructive pattern.

While it's unlikely that we'll ever completely overcome our early influences, we can learn to build around some of these emotional obstacles. One of my clients, Tim, was smart and educated but could never, as he said, "get on top" of his money. As we began to examine his money history, Tim recalled that his parents had always struggled financially. After a number of years, his parents did manage to reach a certain financial stability, but not too long after, Tim's father contracted a serious illness. His father and mother were set back by a considerable sum and never recovered. Tim began to realize how profoundly this had shaped his own behavior with money. The message he had carried into adulthood was, "You had better not be successful or something horrible will happen."

As Tim worked through a process of deep self-examination, he saw that he had repeatedly reached the brink of financial success but that this pattern had then sabotaged him. He would either lose interest, come up against some truly insurmountable obstacle, or change direction entirely. He had never recognized that there might be a connection to his early experience of his parents' financial woes. Knowing this has helped Tim recognize when he is at the danger point with regard to a potential success in his life. This knowledge has helped him develop strategies for navigating around his obstacles so that he can continue to improve financially.

A money history grows out of these basic questions: How did money help you, and how did money hurt you, as you were growing up? How did your mother deal with money? How did your father deal with money? Compiling a money history will help you understand the emotional components of your financial life. You may discover that some of your issues stem from a childhood fear that "there is not enough" or "there will never be enough." You may get in touch with traits or habits you weren't aware of (grandiosity, excessive self-worth, low self-worth, a tendency to hoard or under-earn, and many more), which you have been acting on in your financial life.

Your history will help you connect your current behavior with money to one or more past experiences and identify which areas of your spending plan may need extra watchfulness on your part. For example, if you were deprived of something or neglected as a child, in what areas of your spending today do you continue to act out this early experience (or seek its resolution)?

As you write your money autobiography, make sure you start with the past and move forward. Approach the material chronologically, to mirror the way the belief system itself developed. Writing a money history is a process that has had a profound effect on everyone I've seen who has undertaken the task. It is invaluable for clients to see for the first time where their belief systems and attitudes about money came from. The process can be especially meaningful for couples. In a counseling session, when couples begin to share their memories of money growing up, I can see a dynamic shift as they gain a new understanding of one another and how they are each affected by their money histories. Often this one step alone defuses some of the power struggles they've been engaged in for years.

What is your earliest memory of money? How did it make you feel, and what messages about money do you carry today that might relate to those early feelings?

How do you feel when you think about the state of your financial
life today?

Level One

How do you feel your financial condition affects the way others
see you?

_____

_____

_____

_____

_____

_____

_____

How does your financial condition affect the way you see yourself?

_____

_____

_____

_____

_____

_____

_____

Do your reactions to events in your life make you engage in self-defeating behaviors with money? What would be a typical example?

Was there a time when you had plenty of money in the bank?
Did you have a different feeling about life?

If you were asked whether you have the skills to deal effectively with money, would you answer yes or no? The reasons would be:

How does your financial condition affect your peace of mind?

Reviewing What You've Learned in Level One

You've probably noticed that in the Financial Hierarchy, the level you've just completed is the largest and broadest. While we have only covered the first level of five, I've addressed a number of topics and given you a lot of detail. This business of constructing or reconstructing your financial life is no small job. Level One embodies some of the most difficult work.

So far you have:

* Learned how to manage your checkbook and track your expenses and income, giving you clarity about your overall financial picture and what you do with the money you have

* Created a Monthly Spending Plan that allows you to see the consequences of a spending choice while you can still do something about it

* Developed a plan for debt management/reduction/elimination—another important step in learning to live within your means

* Gotten in touch with some of the emotional contributors to your behaviors with money, giving you the sense of competence and empowerment that usually accompanies the new "take charge" attitude you have toward your financial life

* Discovered ways of building around the obstacles that have kept you from reaching your goals

Having completed Level One, you may feel eager to begin building on what you have done. Or you may want to take some time to learn and refine the new money behaviors that have begun to form the foundation for your financial future. Whatever you are feeling at this point, it is important to continue the building process, since even the best-engineered foundation will eventually become unusable if it is not put to its intended purpose.

In Level Two we will be setting the cornerstones for the rest of your structure. Let's begin.

Level 2

Setting the Cornerstones

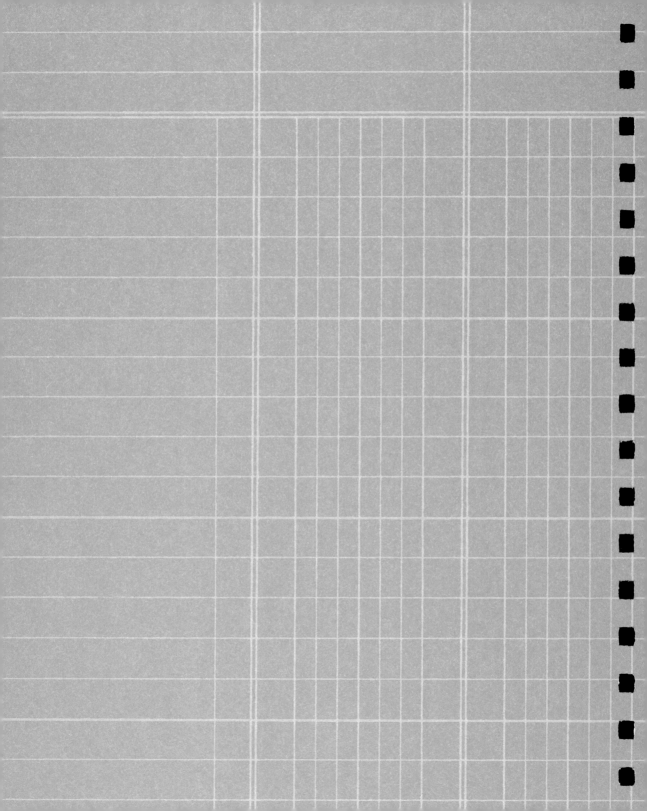

The goal of Level One was to gain clarity and understanding about your financial situation, through the development of some basic sound money behaviors. With these in place, you now have the foundation on which to set the cornerstones of your new financial life: Savings, Insurance, Education, and Action.

In Level Two, you'll be:

* Assessing your savings and learning about the hierarchy of savings

* Making a thorough assessment of your current assets

* Taking a look at insurance—what you have and what you may need

* Exploring the gaps in your financial knowledge—focusing on what you know and what you still need to know in order to move your financial life forward

* Developing an action plan that shows the steps you need to take in order to continue building your financial structure

What we're actually talking about in this section are your safety and security needs—both practical and emotional.

SAVINGS

Why don't people save? Most people have heard about the idea of saving 10 percent of what they make, paying themselves first, or having enough money to cover six months' worth of expenses in the bank. So how can it be that in the midst of some of the most prosperous times the United States has ever known, so many women and men continue to court disaster by having no money set aside as savings?

There are three main obstacles to successful saving:

* You haven't developed the habit of saving

* You have established belief systems about money that prevent you from saving

* You—like so many others—simply procrastinate

One of the biggest reasons people procrastinate is the belief that they can't start saving until they are out of debt. In fact, much of what is written about savings in the popular press advises that if you have any savings, for heaven's sake take the money and use it to pay down (or pay off) your existing credit card debt. And at first, this seems like a smart idea. What sane person would leave money in a savings account that earns 3 percent (or even less) and keep paying on their credit cards at an interest rate of at least 18 percent?

You do this, though, at the risk of running short of money if an unexpected expense comes up–and one always will. What if your car breaks down? What if you are laid off from your job? It happens all the time in this era of mega-mergers and corporate downsizing. And what if you are presented with a grand career opportunity that you're just dying to accept, but you wonder how you'll scrape together the cost of moving halfway across the country so you can take the job?

If you keep some savings in the bank, there's a much better chance that you won't automatically pull out the plastic when there's an emergency or other unanticipated expense, perpetuating your ride on the financial roller coaster.

If you want to stop being in debt, you have to start saving. Many people have simply never developed the habit of saving something regularly each month, even a small amount. While it does take discipline, especially at first, the payoff can be huge. Remember Louise, who had worn down her assets to a fraction of their former amount and had credit card debt of nearly $70,000? When she decided to turn her financial life around, she made a decision that the first thing she'd do every month was take 10 to 15 percent right off the top of everything she earned and sock it away in a savings account. She did this even before calculating her business expenses. More important than the very real financial security her savings provide her with today, though, are the self-esteem and peace of mind she feels at having begun to provide herself with one of the most basic forms of financial protection.

If you put money into a savings account regularly, you will be amazed at what you've managed to accumulate at the end of a year in financial and emotional capital. The feelings of safety and security that begin to form when you put the savings cornerstone in place are profound and can lead to changes in every area of your financial life.

Dave's story is a good example of what can happen when you start saving. A self-employed hairdresser, Dave had never saved a dime. His income was inadequate and didn't allow him any of the extras he liked in his life. He used a fistful of credit cards, supplemented by money that should have gone to paying his quarterly taxes, to maintain a lifestyle closer to the one he really wanted. By the time Dave came to see me, he was juggling his finances with an increasing sense of desperation, and his tangle of unmet financial obligations looked almost insurmountable.

But despair can be a great teacher. Dave stopped overspending and began to live on what he earned. He started paying his current quarterly taxes and worked out a payment plan on his back taxes. He made saving a priority even though he still had a lot of debt to pay off. Slowly Dave's financial life began to shift. As he began taking responsibility for his own financial well-being and his self-esteem increased, he began to take a more active approach to booking appointments with clients—calling them if they hadn't been into the shop for a while and letting them know of openings he had, rather than waiting for the phone to ring. His income began to go up. As he was released from the fear that his financial situation had put him in, his ability to enjoy his work increased. Today, Dave has almost as much business as he can handle and the income to afford the extras that he used to charge. He is current on all his taxes and has begun to consider what kinds of investments he wants to make.

It's true that if you pay off your debts a little at a time, as Dave did, it will take longer to clear that side of your balance sheet. But the payoff you get from knowing that your safety and security needs are being met, in part by having savings in the bank, is worth much more than a few more months spent paying credit card interest.

It's important to understand that, as with other aspects of our financial life, there is a strong emotional component to our feelings about savings. This may continue to impact our behavior long after the original experience has been forgotten. My friend Jenny was raised to believe what generations of her female forebears had believed–that she would one day marry and that her husband would take care of all her financial needs. As it turned out, Jenny didn't marry until late in life and endured years of financial struggle because of her strong attachment to an unrealistic legacy.

Another friend of mine, Bob, tells this story from his childhood: When he was about eight years old, Bob started his own private savings "bank" in the toe of one of his prized Roy Rogers cowboy boots. The boot was hidden deep in his closet. On a regular basis, Bob would add to the shiny coins he had stashed there. He didn't have an immediate plan for his savings. It just felt good to know the money was there.

The money Bob saved had been taken, over a period of time, from the top of his parents' dresser (many of the stories I hear about children's efforts to save money involve "borrowing" of this kind). But when Bob's mother discovered the boot with its stash of coins, she "stole" the money from him, taking it back and admonishing Bob for what he had done. As an adult, Bob began to wonder whether the message conveyed by this early experience might have contributed to his long-standing inability to save.

Bob married and had a son, who had his own negative experience of saving money. Steve wanted a bicycle. At thirteen, he savored the idea of the independence this would give him. But the family was struggling just to make ends meet and couldn't afford the bicycle. So Steve began to save. The money was collected from odd jobs, plus the occasional birthday or holiday gift from relatives and family friends. Finally, the day came when Steve bought his bicycle. Less than a month later, it was stolen. Steve had left the bicycle unlocked on the front porch, in full view of passersby. The incident might have been written off to a teenager's carelessness in

forgetting to lock the bike. But when Bob learned about the loss, he
began to suspect that the belief systems that had dominated his
own behavior with money might have begun to take root in his son.

Let's take a look at some of your emotional drivers.

What is your first memory of saving money?

Where did the money come from?

What did you plan to use the money for?

What happened to your savings?

What's the main belief about saving money that you think you might
have developed as a result of your experience?

What is your relationship to savings now that you're an adult? Are you currently saving money? How much a month?

What are you saving for?

How do you feel whenever you put money into your savings?

What feelings come up for you when you withdraw money from your savings account?

_____

_____

_____

_____

_____

_____

_____

If you don't have any savings right now, how does that make you feel?

_____

_____

_____

_____

_____

_____

_____

_____

Of all the things that can begin to help you change your money-saving behavior, the most important is to learn to look at savings not as a single item but rather as a system similar to the basic financial hierarchy we began to develop in the early parts of this book. There are three separate but interrelated levels of the Hierarchy of Savings:

Periodic Expense Account: Money meant to be spent. This is money you set aside for expenses that you anticipate such as car registration, taxes, membership dues, car repairs, vacations, holidays, etc.

Prudent Reserve Account: Money not to be spent. This is money saved but not spent until or unless it is needed to cover ordinary living expenses in the event of an unanticipated loss of income (being laid off from a job, being unable to work due to injury or illness, etc.).

Investment Savings: Money for the future. This money is for long-term investments and future needs, such as purchasing a home, your children's education, retirement planning, and other long-term goals. It should accumulate until you have enough to invest it (to fund an IRA or purchase shares in a mutual fund, for example). It will then increase through interest, dividend reinvestment, and other tools designed to help you grow your money.

You might want to set up separate accounts for each kind of savings, although many people put all of their savings dollars into one account and set up a system for tracking the amounts allocated to each category.

Let's take a look at what can happen when any of the three pieces of the Hierarchy of Savings is missing.

Bonnie, a successful therapist in private practice, had no periodic savings or prudent reserve. She did, however, have two IRAs she had funded. She felt very good about the fact that she was beginning to plan for the time—still far in the future—when she would retire. One month, however, Bonnie was faced with an unexpected surgery—not serious, but she would be out of work for six weeks and be unable to see clients. Her recovery took a little longer than she and her doctor had anticipated. Bonnie was forced to cash in her IRAs and use the money to live on. Needless to say, she was devastated when she saw that after the taxes and early-withdrawal penalties, her IRAs had shrunk to 50 percent of their value. Her investment program had failed, not because the investments were unsound but because the other two pieces of her savings hierarchy weren't in place.

Let's look at each component in the Hierarchy of Savings in a little more detail.

PERIODIC EXPENSE ACCOUNT

The base of the savings hierarchy is periodic savings, put into a special account for expenses that you know are coming but are not yet due. This helps you avoid the all-too-familiar "cash crunches" and the need to use credit cards or investment savings to meet an obligation you knew was coming. Having periodic savings addresses your safety and security needs at their most basic level.

When my daughter Tammie was just out of college, she called me up one day and asked, "Mom, do you want the bad news or the good news?" Tammie reported that her mechanic had just called to say that her older-model car needed $700 in repairs. That was the bad news. The good news, Tammie exulted, was that she had the money in the bank to pay for the repairs, since some months before she'd begun to set aside money in her periodic expense account for car maintenance.

Another very important category for periodic savings is taxes. People who are self-employed need to save so they'll have the money when quarterly tax payments roll around. Homeowners need to save for the day their property taxes come due. Other categories covered by periodic savings might include large purchases, holiday gift giving, travel to attend an upcoming conference or family occasion, and vacations—a category that two other long-time clients, Tom and Erica, felt they couldn't even consider because of their many other financial obligations. But Tom and Erica began to set aside money for periodic savings and this changed.

This meant they had to curb their impulse spending dramatically. Their initial concern was that they'd feel "deprived" if they couldn't be spontaneous in their spending choices. But being able to take much-needed vacations would be well worth it. Tom and Erica watched their vacation funds build over the course of a year or so, and last summer they were able to fulfill a long-standing promise to their three children. They took a family trip to Disneyland and paid cash for everything. "It was the best feeling in the world," said Tom.

Make a list of what your regular periodic expenses might be and what amount you'd ideally like to set aside for each:

EXPENSE	AMOUNT	MONTH DUE
	$	

Level Two

EXPENSE	AMOUNT	MONTH DUE
	$	

Imagine having your periodic expenses covered for one year. How would that feel?

Having periodic savings will give you two very direct benefits. The first is that you will no longer be driven into new cycles of debt for expenses that you could reasonably have anticipated. Second, when you have provided for these contingencies, you will have an emotional sense that your safety and security are being looked after. Having accomplished this basic level of savings safety, you are ready to develop a reserve of money you will not spend unless there is an interruption in your income.

PRUDENT RESERVE ACCOUNT

Resting on the foundation of your savings for periodic expenses are your prudent reserve savings—the money you've set aside in case you have an unanticipated loss of income due to a job change, illness, or unexpected catastrophic event. Keep in mind that expenses like car repairs are neither catastrophic nor unexpected and belong in your Periodic Expenses savings category.

Most financial planning books suggest a prudent reserve that would cover three to six months of your living expenses. This is a great idea, but for many people it is the financial equivalent of walking to the moon. The first step in determining what you should have in your prudent reserve is to assess your income flow.

If you have a steady job, with little or no chance of losing that job, you may not need to have a six-month reserve. A three-month prudent reserve might be perfectly adequate. Another factor to consider is the function of any disability insurance you may have. Look at the length of time before your disability will kick in—usually it's 30, 60, 90, or even sometimes 120 days—and use that as the basis for figuring out how much of a prudent reserve you should have. Obviously, if your disability insurance won't begin paying out money for 120 days you will want a larger prudent reserve than you would if it kicks in after 30. On the other hand, if you are self-employed or in a profession where your income fluctuates (sales, a commission-based job, or the like), you should have a reserve designed to cover longer periods of interrupted income.

Lack of a prudent reserve put one of my clients, a highly successful real estate agent, on a financial (and emotional) roller coaster. When Stacy first came to see me in 1993, she told me she felt she had "real issues with money," even though she'd been a bookkeeper in her previous career. She had no savings, was living on her credit cards, and had amassed a debt of $43,000 ($13,000 on credit cards and the rest borrowed from friends and family for taxes).

She did well selling high-end properties in one of the country's wealthiest areas. She would sometimes, however, go for months between escrows. So while her commission checks were often substantial, they were irregular. When a check did come in, Stacy would pay all her bills, but there would be nothing left for her to live on.

Stacy had fallen into a debilitating cycle: with no prudent reserve, she supported her lifestyle with credit cards between commission checks. When a check arrived, out the money would go to pay off Stacy's credit cards. With no cash left for living expenses, the cycle would begin anew. She would again pull out the plastic to handle her normal living expenses or take out personal loans from friends.

Stacy and I agreed that our first goal was to take her next large commission check and use it to establish a prudent reserve. We decided that her prudent reserve should be large enough to cover both basic living expenses and periodic expenses for several months. We agreed that Stacy would not use her credit cards to survive on until her next check came in. For the time being, she would make only the minimum payments on her credit cards, and the total of these payments was to be included in her prudent reserve.

Taxes in particular had always been a problem for Stacy. She always paid on time and never incurred penalties and interest, but she borrowed heavily from family and friends in order to do this. So we made sure that Stacy's prudent reserve also provided for payment of all taxes that would come due in the period before she anticipated receiving another check.

The plan worked. When her next commission check came in, Stacy drew just what she needed for that month's living expenses, and used the remainder of the check to establish her prudent reserve. Over the months that followed, each time a new commission check came in, Stacy would draw only what she needed to cover her living expenses. The remainder she used to add to her prudent reserve. The result was that Stacy stopped the chaotic cycle of spend-and-borrow, spend-and-borrow that had dominated her life for so long.

The following questions will help you determine how much of a prudent reserve you should probably have.

If you lost your job, how long do you estimate it would take you to find another one in your field of work?

What additional expenses would you want to provide for (telephone calls, résumé preparation and/or printing, travel, etc.) as part of doing a job search?

Are there any medical or other situations that might cause you to be out of work for a period of time? What is the longest time you might go without income in the event of one of these situations?

What additional expenses might be associated with a medical or other situation that would keep you out of work for a period of time? (If you're single, you might want to travel to be closer to an immediate family member, for example.)

With the insurance you now have, how long would it be before you began receiving disability payments?

Now that you have assessed your need for a prudent reserve, how many months' worth of expenses do you feel your reserve should contain?

Using the expenses you included in your Monthly Spending Plan, write down the total amount of money you need to live on each month. What would it feel like to have a month's worth of expenses covered by a prudent reserve?

Write down the amount you'd need in your prudent reserve to cover three months in expenses. How would it feel to have a three-month prudent reserve in the bank?

Write down what your six-month prudent reserve would be. Describe how it would feel if you had a six-month prudent reserve in the bank.

Now write down what you would need in your prudent reserve to live for a year with no other income. The idea of having a one-year prudent reserve may allow you to envision experiences that you never could have imagined possible before. Write out what opportunities might be opened to you with a prudent reserve of this size.

As you look at your prudent reserve needs, it may feel impossible to ever set aside that amount of money and not touch it unless there's an interruption in your income—especially if you've never saved before. Start small. I suggest taking it in bite-sized pieces. Begin by putting into a prudent reserve savings account what you would need to cover one month's worth of groceries. Next month, add what you would need for your monthly rent or mortgage payment. The month after that, take the amount you pay for utilities each month and add it to your prudent reserve.

Build your prudent reserve in blocks until you have the amount you've determined you need. Remember, the key is that you not touch this money for any reason other than a loss of income. The feelings of safety and security—not to mention the increase in self-esteem that comes from knowing you've done all you can to provide for yourself and your family—will be well worth the effort.

Use this space to write down the amount with which you'll kick off your prudent reserve savings, and what the money will cover. Then list what you'll add in future months and what it can cover:

AMOUNT	DATE	ITEMS AMOUNT WILL COVER
$		

AMOUNT	DATE	ITEMS AMOUNT WILL COVER
$		

INVESTMENT SAVINGS

Savings and investments are two different things. While savings are dollars that are simply being held until you spend them for something, investments are dollars that you put aside with an eye toward increasing your money. Investment saving is a long-range saving strategy that will allow you to increase your money over a period of time to meet future needs, like your children's education or your own retirement.

Stacy, the real estate agent we discussed earlier, was able to stop being in debt once she had established a prudent reserve. She was no longer using her credit cards to live on or borrowing from family and friends to cover emergencies or pay her taxes. Instead of using her commission checks to pay off all the charges she had stacked up on her credit cards, she was putting the better portion of this money into her prudent reserve savings.

With a prudent reserve established, Stacy and I focused on our next goal: beginning to save so that Stacy could invest some of her money. Contrary to the advice of friends who were financial planners, Stacy had not yet paid off all her credit card debt. But instead of paying off her debts and postponing her investment savings indefinitely, we focused on laying the groundwork for her financial future by earmarking some of her money for investment savings. Again, we started small.

Today, Stacy has money in a retirement account, regularly saves a percentage of her income right off the top, has stopped using her credit cards altogether, and is totally out of debt. Stacy had to live with her debt for quite a while, paying it off slowly over a period of time; but she didn't let that stop her from getting on with her financial life.

While initially you might feel that you want to weight your savings more heavily in favor of periodic savings and prudent reserve savings, don't ignore investment savings. When you think of saving for investment, what kinds of things do you want to save for? What do you want the growth of your money to do for you? Make it possible to buy a second home? Give your children a top education? Provide a certain standard of living for you and your family after you've retired?

List your goals here:

Based on what you want your life to look—and feel—like, fill in your own Hierarchy of Savings. In the right-hand portion of each level, fill in what the money saved will cover. In the left-hand segment of each level, write down the amount of money you'd ideally like to put into each kind of savings every month. These amounts will continue to change as your financial circumstances start to shift. If you're starting small, that's just fine. The important thing is to start. Remember that the Hierarchy of Savings is the way you'll begin to build a sturdy, rewarding financial structure and is the key to reducing your reliance on the use of credit.

My Personal Hierarchy of Savings

**Amount I'd like to put
in each month**

**What I'd like the money
saved to cover**

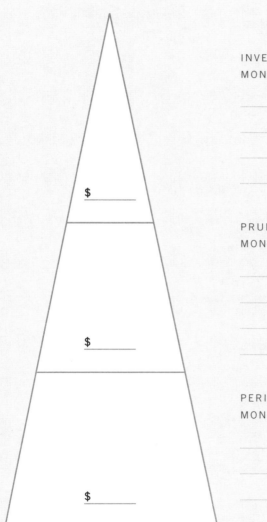

$ _____

$ _____

$ _____

INVESTMENT SAVINGS:
MONEY FOR THE FUTURE

PRUDENT RESERVE ACCOUNT:
MONEY NOT TO BE SPENT

PERIODIC EXPENSE ACCOUNT:
MONEY MEANT TO BE SPENT

INSURANCE

Insurance is a daunting subject. Besides our natural tendency to put off doing things we don't fully understand, most people avoid the whole idea of insurance because it involves topics we'd rather not have to look at. As financial counselor and best-selling author Eric Tyson says in his book *Personal Finance for Dummies,* "Most people associate insurance with disease, death, and disaster and would rather do just about anything other than review or spend money on insurance."

My friends Jana and Paul, parents of eight- and four-year-old girls, are two of the most intelligent and caring people I know. They are devoted to raising their daughters, attending to their physical needs, intellectual life, and spiritual development with passionate interest and love. Yet neither Jana nor Paul (both of whom are self-employed) has either life or disability insurance. This is despite the fact that Jana's father was an insurance salesman and Jana was raised in an environment where insurance was a valued priority.

Clients and friends often rationalize not getting insurance by saying that if they have insurance "it will just draw disaster" to them. Others say, "It's just too expensive." Whatever the reason, increasing numbers of Americans are uninsured or underinsured; according to the nonprofit National Insurance Consumer Organization, nine out of ten Americans purchase the wrong kinds and amounts of insurance.

Insurance is one of the most important pieces of your financial life. For one thing, you can build savings and investments, buy houses, and have a great job, but without proper insurance coverage—selected and paid for in the hope you'll never need it—you can lose it all instantly. When I work with clients, one thing we look at very early on is whether or not they have insurance. One of my clients came to see me just after the devastating fire in the hills of Oakland, California, in 1991. Denise's home was in the fire area. As she and her little girl fled from the flames, the only things they took with them were Denise's important papers, family photographs, and her daughter's Halloween costume. Denise described the "strange sense of calm that overtook me as we drove away. I knew we were adequately insured for the loss of our home and everything in it. And anyway, I knew I was already taking my most precious assets with me—everything else could be replaced."

Another testament to both the practical and emotional value of having the proper insurance was something I read just recently in my local newspaper. The story focused on a woman whose husband, a forty-nine-year-old attorney, had died unexpectedly of a heart attack, leaving her and their four young children. The man had, however, had the foresight to provide not only adequate life insurance, but even mortgage insurance (he was the family's sole provider) that covered the unpaid balance on the home they had lived in for many years. His widow told the newspaper, "My husband often told me how much peace of mind it gave him to know that we were protected if anything happened to him. There's not a day that goes by that I don't thank that dear man for loving us enough to make sure we were cared for."

Feeling that we and our loved ones, and the other things that are most valuable to us, are protected and safe is one of our most basic psychological needs. Whether we're aware of it or not, when this deep need goes unmet, the fear and anxiety that take root can undermine our sense of well-being, our self-esteem, our quality of life itself.

How have you provided for your protection in case of illness or accident? If you have no insurance protection, how do you anticipate taking care of yourself if you become ill or have an accident? When you think about this, what feelings come up for you?

How have you provided protection for your loved ones in case of your death or disability? If you haven't provided for them, how do you feel about it?

How have you provided for protection of your assets in case of a
disaster or lawsuit?

Have you had an experience in your life when insurance worked well
(an illness or early death in the family, for example)? Describe how
insurance worked for the people involved.

Was there a time in your life when insurance would have been useful? Describe what it was like not to have insurance.

No matter how careful and thoughtful you are, there are things you can't plan for. Failing to provide for the unanticipated things in life—no matter how unlikely they seem—leads to both external and internal instabilities that can eventually undermine your entire financial structure. Even when you're in a position where you have saved money for unforeseen expenses, the right kind of insurance (focusing first on the things that could really wipe you out financially) is equally important. A failure to provide for the uncertainties of life—for the unknown, and unknowable—can come at a very high price. As my wise friend David Shore says, "A successful person embraces life's unpredictability."

Imagine that you're my client and we're sitting in my office. I've asked you if you have disability insurance and you've told me you don't. Please tell me why.

Now I'd like you to imagine sitting in front of your young son or daughter (or any loved one who is dependent upon you). Tell them about your life insurance: Do you have it? Tell them how you chose the amount of life insurance you have. If you have no life insurance, explain to them why not.

Here's an exercise just for you. If you don't have health insurance, I'd like you to stand in front of the mirror, look directly into your own eyes, and tell yourself how you'll take care of yourself if you suffer an illness or have an accident. Write down what you say and feel here.

The point of these exercises is to get you in touch with the fact that insurance can be an emotionally charged topic. And emotional obstacles aside, the subject of insurance can be very complex.

Take a minute to assess where you stand with the most basic kinds of insurance:

TYPES OF INSURANCE:

	HAVE	NEED
Personal		
Health	○	○
Life	○	○
Income	○	○
Property		
Home	○	○
Auto	○	○
Liability		
Home	○	○
Auto	○	○
Business		
Malpractice	○	○
Workers Compensation	○	○

In the next two sections of your journal, you'll be working on the last two cornerstones of your new financial structure: developing the ability to educate yourself about financial matters—whether it's insurance, stocks, or retirement planning—and creating a plan of action.

EDUCATION

The most important thing you can do to improve your financial situation is develop your financial knowledge. As Barbara Stanny, author of *Prince Charming Isn't Coming*, says: "Money doesn't give you security and power; understanding money gives you security and power." Yet for many people, the very words "financial education" conjure up a certain kind of dread and bring forth images of long, boring books on economics.

When I took my first financial planning class a number of years ago, I found myself drifting away during certain parts of the presentation. Despite my best intentions, I just couldn't stay with the process. I wanted to learn; that certainly wasn't the problem. I attended every class. I asked questions. I did my homework. Yet in almost every session, there would come a time when my eyes would begin to glaze over, my limbs would grow heavy, and I would sink into a stupor. I remained in this state until something—a particularly lively exchange between class members, or a break in the class—brought me back to the surface, and I was able to rejoin the class.

Needless to say, I didn't learn much about financial planning in that class. But to this day I do remember how uncomfortable the experience was. So when I began teaching my own clients and students about planning their financial futures, I knew I wanted to come up with a way to help them create a different experience for themselves. I was keenly aware that, for many people, talking about money can feel overwhelming. The subject of money also often triggers conscious or unconscious emotional issues that can distract us from the topic at hand. I wanted my students to be able to be fully engaged with the material we'd be covering in class.

One day an idea sprang to mind: what if my students could be encouraged to alert me whenever they became distracted or confused, say by using a bell. Many of the world's great religions have used the ringing of a bell as a kind of "call to consciousness"—as both an invitation to the process itself and as a reminder to stay in the moment as events unfold. Would this work for the students in my classes?

When participants arrived for my next class, at each student's seat was a bell. It could have been any kind of bell, but the type I happened to use was one of those inexpensive, wonderfully utilitarian bells that you might see on the counter at the dry cleaner's or the deli along with a sign that says, "Ring Bell for Service."

I instructed my students to ring their bells any time they felt themselves about to "glaze over"—any time the complexity of the material or the triggering of an emotional issue made it hard for them to stay with the class. To encourage class members to use their bells freely, I offered a prize to the person who summoned the courage to ring the bell most often. My goal was to encourage students to feel good about asking questions, good about using their confusion as an opportunity to deepen the learning process.

In that initial class, bells started ringing almost at once, as my students struggled to take in new information and embrace new ways of thinking about their financial lives. At first the bells inspired a bit of uncomfortable laughter. But the bell ringing worked, and the class quickly adopted this way of "calling them- selves back" to our shared process. What I began to notice, as the course progressed, was that there was a pattern to the ringing. For example, beginning discussion of a topic that represented taking another step up on the scale of financial maturity always inspired lots of bell ringing. Each time a bell rang, I would ask the student, "What's the last thing you remember?" And together we would go from there, working to identify exactly what feelings had triggered the student's response.

Simple? Yes. But it was (and remains) very effective for my clients and students, and it warms me profoundly each time I see a student abandon that feeling of intimidation and embrace our fun- damental right not to know everything. As you begin developing your financial knowledge, I'd like to encourage you to find a bell–

any size or kind will do—to keep by your side as you go. Ring the bell as frequently as you need to in order to keep yourself in the process and alive to the possibilities offered by what you're learning.

I can't emphasize strongly enough how necessary it is for you to take charge of your own financial planning process. I don't mean that you have to have a stockbroker's knowledge of stocks, a Certified Financial Planner's knowledge of investments, or an attorney's knowledge of trusts and wills. What I am saying is that it's critically important for you to be involved in the process of planning your financial life.

Many of my clients want to just skip the education piece of the work and say, "I am going to go to a professional financial planner who has all the knowledge. If I turn it over to my planner, why should I bother myself with it?" On the surface, this seems a pretty logical course of action. But even for those of you who do plan to turn your financial planning over to a professional, if you're not educated enough to understand what your planner is doing for you, you will be removed from the process in such a way that—unless you're just lucky—your success will be haphazard at best.

Your ability to assess the relative worth of the professionals you work with can help you avoid situations like the one that Northern California newspapers splashed across their front pages late in 1997. This story was about an investment advisor who had stolen millions of dollars from his clients' life savings. The media reported that he had allegedly forged at least one client's signature, falsely represented the value of an insurance policy, and perpetrated a number of other frauds.

When I read that story, even though my heart went out to those who had lost all their money, my sympathy was tempered by my belief that a lot of the responsibility lay with the victims themselves. Why? Because with just two phone calls, they could have discovered that the advisor had records of violations going back a number of years, had been fined by the National Association of Securities Dealers, and had been barred by the California Department of Corporations from "any position of employment, management, or

control of any broker-dealer or investment advisor in California."
Your willingness to educate yourself reduces your chances of being
a victim and increases your chance of being a victor.

While the idea of having to take responsibility for your financial knowledge may seem unconquerable at first, I can assure you
that it is a key to your building and maintaining a solid financial
structure. And it's not too hard to do if you take it in nice, small,
bite-sized chunks.

Your financial education can be broken down into three main
areas–The Three Ps:

Principles   •   Professionals   •   Products

Understanding some basic principles of finance will give you
the ability to understand how different products and professionals
can be used to achieve your short- and long-term financial goals. A
working knowledge of the roles different professionals can play in
your planning will allow you to assess whether or not you need
their services. As you begin to fill the gaps in your knowledge of
financial products and services, this new information will add
strength and integrity to your financial structure. You can begin
your education process simply by identifying the gaps in your
knowledge.

How would you characterize your knowledge of the following areas:

	KNOWLEDGEABLE	SOMEWHAT KNOWLEDGEABLE	NOT A CLUE
Savings	○	○	○
Insurance	○	○	○
Taxes	○	○	○
Investments	○	○	○
Employee Benefits	○	○	○
Estate Planning	○	○	○

What specific thoughts, emotions, or attitudes come up for you when you think about increasing your knowledge of financial planning?

_____

_____

_____

_____

_____

_____

_____

When you think about the things you need to learn, what topics feel
the most confusing?

What have you done so far toward your financial planning education?

Of these, what was the most effective thing that you have done? Why? The least effective? Why?

There may be wide gaps in your knowledge of financial planning. You may feel like walking off into the sunset ringing your bell. Don't be discouraged. My clients who have decided to become "students" of financial planning have, without exception, found the process intellectually stimulating, emotionally satisfying, and, most of all, personally empowering. One woman who took one of my classes in personal financial planning—a student who'd begun the six-week course saying she felt "vague and fearful" about our topic—wrote me later that she felt "grounded, interested in incorporating long-term thinking into my consciousness and vocabulary, and concerned, for the very first time, about my own security and financial well-being."

Remember that learning is a lifelong process; you won't learn everything you hope to know all at once. As you continue to expand your financial structure, you will need to keep adding to your knowledge of matters that will apply to your own financial life. By doing this you will become aware of new tools to help you accomplish the goals you have set out and see how new ideas integrate with your existing plan.

During our honeymoon in London, my husband and I loved riding London's underground transit system. One of the things we'll always remember is the very British-sounding voice coming through the loudspeaker politely reminding all patrons to "mind the gap"– there was a space of about a foot between the edge of the train platform and the train itself.

As you look back over what you have done in these last pages, I'd like you to regard each of the "gaps" in your knowledge of financial planning, and decide which you need to "mind" first.

My knowledge gaps, in order of importance:

When you're ready, let's begin to develop a plan of action for your financial life.

ACTION

Whatever you can do or dream you can, begin it.
Boldness has genius, power, and magic in it.
—Goethe

Now we're going to set in place the final cornerstone of your new financial structure: action. In many ways this is the most important piece of your financial hierarchy's second level, because in order to carry out a financial plan, at some point you are going to have to take action.

In my classes, it's usually right about now that my students drown out my voice with a cacophony of bell ringing. People really do get afraid at this point. It may be that they're afraid they won't seem "smart." It may be that they're fearful of acting lest they "do the wrong thing." It may be a gnawing sense that financial matters are better left to "someone more qualified."

I'll tell you the same thing I tell my students: If you're going to develop a sound financial structure, you will need to find a way to span the ground that lies between your newly forming ideas about financial planning and the inertia you feel when you contemplate acting on them. And I've found that the most effective way to make the leap is to identify how you feel when you contemplate taking an action and pick one item or area to start with. Just as you found earlier in some of the other aspects of your financial structure, there also may be a strong underlying emotional component to the actions–or the lack of actions–in your financial life.

As you contemplate taking action in your financial life, describe the
thoughts, feelings, and memories that come to you.

One of the major blocks that people have in terms of taking action in their financial lives is trying to do the things they think they should do, rather than the things they want to do. I encourage you to begin with the things you want to do, the things that make you excited about learning. Kathleen Mitchell, Ed.D., a career counselor at City College of San Francisco, says, "We have lost our ability to be curious." And while we often tell ourselves that it's the constraints of time, money, or physical and emotional stamina that prevent us from pursuing what interests us, my experience is that what stops most people is the lack of permission we give ourselves to be curious.

But it is curiosity that makes us teachable. It is a sense of curiosity that draws us forward into taking the actions needed in our lives. Look back over your list of knowledge gaps and focus on the areas that seem to exert a special pull. When you consider learning new things, which things on your list make you feel excited? Which things fire your imagination?

Go back to the assessment of your financial knowledge that you made on page 123. Pick the knowledge gap that you are the most curious about and write it down here:

Now take a minute and think about how your life would look if you were able to take action in this area. Describe how your life would be affected in positive ways.

Let's turn the tables: Describe what your life would look like if you
don't find a way to take action in this area.

By now you're probably beginning to get an idea of how taking action in your financial life could transform your life overall. But you may still be finding it difficult to move forward. You're not alone. Over the years, I've watched clients and students struggle at this stage of their financial journey, blocked by the immensity of the undertaking or the seeming impossibility of the final results they hope to achieve—unable to take even the smallest step. But the smallest step is exactly the right place to begin.

Some years ago, after my practice was well established, I was involved in an automobile accident. This heightened my desire to do something about providing more adequate protection for myself—and the people in my life who counted on me—if I became unable to work for any reason. I'd just been rejected for the third time for disability insurance because of a prior medical condition, and I was feeling incredibly responsible for those around me, incredibly vulnerable, and incredibly overwhelmed about what to do first.

A few days later, the idea occurred to me that I already had something that could potentially provide me with income even in the event that I couldn't work. It was the *Financial Recovery Workbook* I'd written (and which my clients continue to use to this day). When it came to doing anything with this insight, though, I didn't know how or where to start. A friend suggested one day that I make one phone call—just one, not a whole string of them—to explore who might be interested in buying the book in quantity.

I took her advice. When I got home, I made my one call to the family support service division of a branch of the U.S. military. The result was a large initial order, with a promise of more to come. I was also hired to present some special training classes. This led to other opportunities and greater public interest in the book. I was reminded, once again, of the power that a single action can have.

Go back to the knowledge gap that you wrote down a minute ago, the one that made you feel curious. Whatever it is, think of a single action you could take that would move you along toward the financial goals you've begun to define.

Write down the action here:

_____

_____

_____

_____

_____

_____

_____

_____

Many of the action steps you identify will involve education, gaining financial knowledge that you'll then use as you continue to build your financial structure. A lot of people imagine that they have to go out and talk to a stockbroker, take a class, or spend hours in a research library. All these things can be useful, depending on what you want to know. But educating yourself can begin with simply gathering information together–your current insurance policies, for example–or phoning a friend who's a financial whiz, or reading that great book on a finance-related subject that has just come out in paperback. Don't make it harder than it has to be. The important thing in educating yourself is finding a way of learning that works for you.

Everybody has a different learning style, and I encourage you to go back over the learning experiences in your life and define the elements of your personal learning style. Do you learn best from a book, or is a classroom setting more effective for you?

What is the best learning experience you ever had? What was
the setting like? What tools did you use? Why was the experience
so effective?

What was your worst learning experience? What was the setting like? In what ways was this experience different from the good learning experience you just described?

The process of identifying what you are drawn to about a subject, picking out just one thing to do, and then taking that one action, will help you begin to develop the habit of taking action in your financial life. This will take time. Your new financial structure won't be built in a day. But do not ignore the importance of this cornerstone. Without this cornerstone in place, you can find yourself being reactive instead of active. You're much more likely to make financial decisions rashly and out of context, and this can cost you dearly.

One of my clients, for example, was a self-employed man in his late forties who had managed to sock away $15,000 in an IRA—his only savings. Perry's inertia around the subject of financial planning continued to block him from taking any action. That's not to say that he wasn't thinking about taking action; he was, constantly. He just couldn't manage to actually do anything.

One day, a golfing buddy came to Perry with a plan: "Give me $15,000, and I'll double it in a few months." Even though Perry knew nothing about the kind of investment his friend was proposing, and instead of educating himself to see how it would fit in with an overall plan of saving and investing, he trusted his friend to "take care of him." He withdrew all the money in his IRA and turned it over to his friend.

His friend's grand plan went belly-up. Perry not only lost his money but also had to pay taxes and early-withdrawal penalties on money he'd never get to use. The lesson is simple. You must act if things are to change, but your actions must be based upon sound financial cornerstones to ensure that you get the results you want.

CREATING YOUR ACTION PLAN

The key to action is to identify your knowledge gaps, then decide on one step that will move you along in your learning process. When it's completed, that step will lead you to the step that follows.

Use this space to write your action plan. In the left-hand column, write each knowledge gap that you identified earlier. To the right of each item on your list, write down what your first step will be.

KNOWLEDGE GAPS   FIRST ACTION STEP

Reviewing What You've Learned in Level Two

By now you have gained clarity around your safety and security needs, identified areas where you need to have more knowledge, and begun an action plan. You're really on your way!

In Level Two you have explored the four cornerstones of your financial hierarchy and:

* Learned about the Hierarchy of Savings and why having savings is so important to your overall structure

* Started getting clearer on your savings needs at both the practical and the emotional levels, which can relieve financial stress and increase your confidence and self-esteem about your financial life

* Learned about assessing your insurance needs and explored the practical and emotional value of having proper insurance

* Discovered where the gaps in your knowledge lie, and what information you need to gather so that you can make appropriate changes to your insurance or any other safety/security issues

* Developed your approach to taking action and discovered the steps you need to take to set your cornerstones firmly in place

* Begun to take action

You begin feeling a freedom from fear and are ready to move on to Level Three and the task of framing your new financial life.

Level **3**

Building the

Framework

In Level One, you laid the foundation for your new financial structure by identifying and addressing some of your most basic needs. In Level Two, you set the cornerstones of your structure in place, examining the practical and emotional value of meeting your safety and security needs, identifying gaps in your financial knowledge, and beginning to take some action. Ideally, by now you've gained a sense of clarity about your money and are beginning to feel there is an order to it all.

In Level Three, we're going to expand on the work you've done and erect the framework of your new financial structure. The rest of your financial life will form itself around the shape that you give to the frame. The work you do in this level will begin to show you how your new financial life is really going to look.

CLARIFYING YOUR VALUES

Many people have the fantasy that if they strive for, and achieve, a certain financial or material state, everything's going to be okay. For most of us, this idea is based on a lack of clarity about what money can and can't do for us. This confusion leads us to behave in ways that aren't consistent with our values, that keep us out of touch with what's really important to us.

My client Allie, for example, came to her appointment one day and announced that she was thinking about buying a used car that a friend had just told her was for sale. She had it all planned out: she would pay cash, using her savings plus $1,000 that her partner had agreed to lend her. Not once in our months of working together had the idea of buying a car come up. I reminded Allie that she'd said she had two big goals for that year: to establish a prudent reserve and to begin investing. We looked at how buying a car stacked up against the sense of self-esteem and inner calm she had been feeling as her savings increased. We also discussed her excitement as the day she'd be able to fund her first IRA drew closer. At her next session, Allie reported she'd decided against the car after all. "When I thought about it, I was able to remember what's really important to me," she told me. "I realized that putting my money towards the goals I've set, instead of buying a car on the spur of the moment, was making a strong choice—one that had a connection to my values."

Nora and Sam also had to do some soul-searching. They are a successful professional couple in their early forties who both work at demanding jobs. When they first came to see me, they told me one of the things they most wanted was to take a real vacation. Because Nora and Sam worked long hours, they were spending around $250 a week eating out. I asked them to imagine what it would feel like to put $150 of that amount each week toward their dream vacation, instead of continuing to fritter away money on meals they were too exhausted to enjoy anyway. When they stopped to think about it, they agreed that a genuine holiday would be far more restorative than hurried meals in restaurants. Several months later, I got a postcard from the small island retreat they'd decided on for their vacation. They, like Allie, had gotten back in touch with what was really important to them.

As you work through Level Three, remember that the framework is the skeleton that holds the financial structure together. For the framework to be sturdy, you have to make strong financial choices. In order to make these choices you must have clarity about what's important to you.

Take a look at your lifestyle. What things in your life really matter to you?

Level Three

What are some of the values you would like to live by? What circumstances and/or money behaviors have kept you from living according to these values?

VALUES I WANT TO LIVE BY

THINGS THAT HAVE PREVENTED ME
FROM LIVING BY MY TRUE VALUES

Without conscious contemplation on your part, confusion about what money can and can't provide will block your awareness of your real values. The ability to achieve what you want out of life will continue to elude you. Your goal is to find out what it is that's truly important to you, so you can learn to make strong choices based on a set of values that support what you want to do with your life. With my clients, what I see over and over again are two important, and related, principles at work:

* When they have clarity about their values, they make different choices about what they do with their money

* As they become more conscious of what they are doing with money, their essential life values become clearer

If you take the time to build your awareness of what matters to you, you will find that you're beginning to meet your needs in more appropriate and fulfilling ways.

ASSESSING WHAT'S IMPORTANT

Let me tell you about a client of mine named Matt, a master gardener with many clients in his prosperous suburban location. He came to his appointment one day after he had received $20,000 as an inheritance. Matt promptly announced his decision to buy a new truck. "My old one is falling apart," he argued. "It needs at least $2,000 in repairs, and it's just not worth it to have the work done. Besides," he continued, "with the kinds of upscale clients I have, I don't like to be driving around in an old rust bucket."

I suggested to Matt that he put off buying the new truck for two months and that he not spend any of his inheritance right away. After a little cajoling, he agreed. I explained to Matt that as we worked together, we'd be examining the things in his life that were important to him and that this process would actually help clarify what he wanted to do about a new truck.

Over the next couple of weeks, we talked about the things that mattered to Matt. We discussed how he had been meeting his essential needs. We looked at the issue of transportation and explored what he really needed in a truck. I asked Matt about housing: he told me that within the next six to eight months he needed to do some minor repairs on the old house he owned. We talked about Matt's business and what needed attention–he hoped to do some promotion to expand his landscape gardening company and wanted to have some professional marketing materials produced. We talked about the future and about the way his lack of attention to any kind of tax, retirement, or other financial planning had affected his feelings of security and self-esteem. "I'm forty-eight years old," he admitted, "and the nagging worry and sense of incompetence dog me every single day."

Matt came to his next session looking happy and relieved. "I figured out what I want to do about buying a truck," he told me. "What did you decide?" I asked him. "I'm going to buy a newer used truck," he said, "and I'm going to pay cash instead of using long-term financing. That way, I'll be meeting my transportation needs in a way that feels better, but I can still make the repairs on my house and expand my business. And," he added with a twinkle in his eye, "maybe I'll use the money I would have spent on monthly truck payments to increase the money I put into my savings account so I can start investing soon."

In helping Matt go through the process of determining what was really important to him, we made use of a tool that was already familiar to him: we developed an Annual Spending Plan, an expanded version of the Monthly Spending Plan. Using the context provided by his Annual Spending Plan, and the values that had become clear to him during the process of creating it, Matt found a way to meet his essential financial needs, realize some important personal and business goals, and still have the funds to begin planning for his future.

Matt discovered the benefits of having a long-range plan, as opposed to his old way of doing things, which was to plan ahead only as far as the end of the month. Having an Annual Spending Plan is the difference between looking at the ocean through the porthole of a ship (which gives you a limited view of one small patch of ocean at a time) and seeing the ocean through the picture window of a house on the beach, which offers you the scope and perspective of the much larger scene. Matt's decision to buy a used truck instead of a new one came about when he truly examined what mattered to him not in just one area–transportation–but in every part of his life.

Now, using what you've learned about what really matters to you, I'd like you to create an annual spending plan of your own.

CREATING YOUR ANNUAL SPENDING PLAN

Just as the Monthly Spending Plan we developed in Level One of this book helped you determine how you would spend your money on a monthly basis and examine the consequences of certain actions before you took them, the Annual Spending Plan helps you to explore the consequences of your spending over a longer period. My clients Mary Beth and Jimmy have regular money meetings during which they record their daily expenses, total their spending in each of the money categories they've developed, and do their monthly spending plan. (I hope that by now you, too, are doing this regularly.) And when it comes to doing their annual plan, they make a special occasion of it. Because of the importance they attach to their Annual Spending Plan, a few years ago they began a New Year's Day ritual that has become an important tradition. Last year, they packed a picnic, some sharp pencils, blank paper and the previous year's plan, and a warm blanket and drove to the beach to have their meeting.

They always begin work on their annual plan by talking about the year ahead–their dreams, their goals, the things they need and want to spend money on–and they commit to paper the money they will be earning and spending in various categories over the course of the year. Among the expenses they record are savings for the house they hope to buy in a year or two. They also allot a certain amount to periodic savings, prudent reserve savings, and investments.

And in areas where they have to choose one way of using their money over another, they told me recently, "We never have the feeling that anything has been taken away. Far from it. We only feel a tremendous sense of freedom that comes from being able to make conscious choices about the ways we spend our money."

INSTRUCTIONS FOR CREATING YOUR ANNUAL SPENDING PLAN

You'll find that mapping out your Annual Spending Plan is simply an extension of the work you did to create your Monthly Spending Plan. But your Annual Spending Plan will provide you a longer-range picture of your financial life by:

*   Providing a place for you to list all your wants, needs, and desires for the year, giving you clarity about what you want to accomplish over a twelve-month period and a grounded basis for long-term decision making in your financial life

*   Functioning as an important tool for setting realistic savings and investment goals, ensuring that these important safety/security needs don't get ignored as you plan your financial year

*   Allowing you to see ahead of time how your spending choices over the course of an entire year can impact your life and showing you where and when you need to make corrections to ensure that you get the results you want

The Annual Spending Plan is a powerful tool for taking charge of your life.

Keep your tools simple.

It may be tempting to use a computer for creating your plan, but I encourage you to use paper and pencil instead. The physical act of writing is an important way of staying connected to the process. Later, once you have a format for your plan, you might want to create your basic form on the computer, but I'd still suggest filling in the numbers by hand.

Do research if you need to.

In doing your plan, you may find that you don't have all the information you need to put accurate figures in every category. You may know that you want to have your car detailed two months from now, for example, but you aren't sure exactly what it will cost you. Make some calls and find out. Remember, clarity is your goal, and "guesstimating" the cost of items in your annual plan defeats your purpose.

Write down all your expenses for the year.

Use your monthly plan as a guide in anticipating your annual expenses. Be sure to include all three savings categories: periodic savings for expenses that come up once or twice a year, prudent reserve savings for protection in case your income is interrupted, and investment savings.

Here is what the Self Care and Transportation Categories might look like in an Annual Spending Plan, including adjustments:

Sample Annual Spending Plan—Self Care

CATEGORY/EXPENSE	FULL-YEAR PLAN	ADJUSTMENTS	ADJUSTED PLAN
SELF CARE			
Toiletries	$ 204	$ -75	$ 129
Haircuts/Coloring/Perms	600	-100	500
Massage/Body Work	600	-300	300
Health Club/Yoga	516		516
Manicure/Pedicure	300	-150	150
Facial/Skin Care	250	-50	200
Cosmetics	240	-40	200
TOTAL SELF CARE	2710	-715	1995

Sample Annual Spending Plan — TRANSPORTATION

CATEGORY/EXPENSE	FULL-YEAR PLAN	ADJUSTMENTS	ADJUSTED PLAN
TRANSPORTATION			
Car Payment/Rental	$ 3900	$	$ 3900
Insurance	1260		1260
Registration	300		300
Gas	1380		1380
Maintenance (oil & lube)	250		250
Repairs			
Car Wash/Detail	500	-250	250
Parking/Tolls	1440	-375	1065
Tickets			
Public Transportation		+100	100
TOTAL TRANSPORTATION	9030	-525	8505

Your Annual Spending Plan

CATEGORY/EXPENSE	FULL-YEAR PLAN	ADJUSTMENTS	ADJUSTED PLAN
	$	$(+/-)	$

CATEGORY/EXPENSE	FULL-YEAR PLAN	ADJUSTMENTS	ADJUSTED PLAN
	$	$(+/-)	$

CATEGORY/EXPENSE	FULL-YEAR PLAN	ADJUSTMENTS	ADJUSTED PLAN
	$	$(+/-)	$

149

Level Three

CATEGORY/EXPENSE	FULL-YEAR PLAN	ADJUSTMENTS	ADJUSTED PLAN
	$	$(+/-)	$

CATEGORY/EXPENSE	FULL-YEAR PLAN	ADJUSTMENTS	ADJUSTED PLAN
	$	$(+/-)	$

Level Three

CATEGORY/EXPENSE	FULL-YEAR PLAN	ADJUSTMENTS	ADJUSTED PLAN
	$	$(+/-)	$

CATEGORY/EXPENSE	FULL-YEAR PLAN	ADJUSTMENTS	ADJUSTED PLAN
	$	$(+/-)	$

CATEGORY/EXPENSE	FULL-YEAR PLAN	ADJUSTMENTS	ADJUSTED PLAN
	$	$(+/-)	$
Total Annual Expenses	$	$(+/-)	$
Total Annual Income			

Don't add up your total expenses categories just yet. Instead, write down here the yearly income you think you would need to earn in order to accomplish the items reflected in your Annual Spending Plan:

$ _____

Now go back and add up your total expenses: $ _____

Subtract your total expenses from the amount you estimated you'd need to earn in order to implement this plan. What is the difference between the two (plus or minus)?

$ _____

What is the difference between your expenses and the amount you currently earn (plus or minus)?

$ _____

How do you feel when you look at the difference between what your plan says you need to spend, and your current income?

_____

_____

_____

_____

_____

_____

Level Three

REFINING YOUR ANNUAL SPENDING PLAN

Once you have listed all your anticipated expenses and all your anticipated income, if your expenses exceed your income, you will go through a process similar to the one you used to adjust your Monthly Spending Plan. Just as Matt discovered what was really important to him as he worked on his annual plan, you, too, will find it easier to prioritize your needs as you take the time to reacquaint yourself with the things that truly matter to you.

As you begin the process of modifying your annual plan, I want you to take a good, long look at it to make sure you have:

* Provided adequately for your essential needs

* Addressed all your safety and security needs

* Allocated money for your savings hierarchy

* Provided for expenses that enhance your lifestyle

One of the biggest values in having an Annual Spending Plan is that it shows you the "big picture." It allows you to look at the way your money is used not only in the context of your daily life but also in relation to both your short- and long-term needs and goals. With the process of values clarification that you've begun, you'll find that the refinements to your Annual Spending Plan are both driven by and continue to help you clarify what is really important to you.

FINDING MONEY FOR SAVING AND INVESTING

On a very practical level, an additional purpose of the Annual Spending Plan is to help you locate dollars (or additional dollars) for saving and investing. One of the first areas I always ask people to examine is their "impulse spending"—the spending that we do on the spur of the moment or simply out of habit. One couple I know managed to save an additional $2,100 over the course of a single year in just this way. Marnie cut out her weekly manicure at $25 a visit, for an annual savings of $1,200. Stuart cut back on the number of automobile magazines he bought each month, shaving off $30 in this category for annual savings of $360. Together,

Marnie and Stu made the decision to buy paperback books instead of hard cover, which saved them $540 a year.

Think back to the impulse buys we identified in Level Two and to the examples of how much can be saved each year just by curbing this unplanned spending. Identify some of your own most common impulse buys and list them here.

How much are these purchases costing you a month on average? How much could you save in a year if you curbed your impulse spending?

IMPULSE ITEM	AVERAGE COST	AMOUNT I COULD SAVE PER YEAR
	$	$

Now, for each item I would like you to answer two questions:

ITEM	WILL HAVING THIS ITEM CHANGE MY LIFE FOR THE BETTER?	WILL MY LIFE BE AFFECTED IF I DON'T HAVE THIS ITEM?

How could I spend this money in a way that better meets my
true needs?

Time and time again I see the magic that exists in this process:

* Look at your overall goals before you spend

* Take time for a reality check and examine how your money behavior relates to your values

* Refine your behavior so that it is connected to the things that matter most to you

By following these steps, you will be able to transform your financial life and change the course of your financial future.

MAKING THE DECISION TO EARN MORE

Another issue that arises in the process of balancing an Annual Spending Plan when expenses exceed current income is whether to earn more. For instance, my client Doreen was an attorney who had struggled for years in her own practice, not keeping very good track of her hours, not following up for repeat business, not paying attention to office expenses. After we had been working together awhile, she sat down and did an Annual Spending Plan. As is often the case, the things Doreen wanted to include exceeded her current income level. So we took some time and found ways to keep certain things, although we had to eliminate others. But something had shifted for Doreen. Having reconnected with her values—the things that mattered to her in life—she realized that she was unwilling to cut anything else from her annual plan, unwilling to "do without."

With her first annual plan under her belt, she could see exactly what it would take to live the life she wanted to have. She now knew that her ideal financial life was not some mysterious figure that would always be slightly beyond her grasp. She realized that the only way she could accomplish what she wanted to do was to increase her income. Armed with this information, she began to focus on her business in a different way.

It's been two years since Doreen did her first annual plan. In that time, she has worked to become much more conscientious about her business practices, especially in following up on potential repeat business and with referrals. Today she is making three times as much as she was the year of that first plan. The moral of the story: refining your Annual Spending Plan is not always about spending less; sometimes it's about earning more. You might find you want to look at one, or both, ways of refining your annual plan.

Reviewing What You've Learned in Level Three

You have now erected the framework of your new financial life, shaped by your true values and strong enough to support the rest of your structure.

In Level Three you have:

* Begun to clarify your values and started to understand what is really meaningful to you in your life

* Gained a new understanding of how values drive your spending choices, and started to define some new values for yourself

* Created an Annual Spending Plan—a sound blueprint for your year's spending and a framework for making adjustments in your spending categories if necessary

* Learned how curbing impulse spending can help you find additional dollars for investing, and started to get a sense of the possibilities your financial life has for you

* Begun to think about whether you want to spend less or earn more, so you're taking charge of your life

Now let's step up to Level Four, where you'll be examining money in relation to the other people in your life.

Level **4**

Bricks

and Mortar

Now the structure of your new financial life is really coming together. But if it is to stand up to the passing years and to the various forces that will buffet it, the frame you've constructed will need sturdy walls that are reinforced at every key point. Up until now, we have been concerned primarily with your relationship to money–how you spend it, how you earn it, how you save it. In Level Four we're going to expand our focus a bit to:

* Examine how your relationship to money can affect those around you

* Look at the ways those around you can affect your financial life

* Discuss how financial professionals can help you solidify your new financial structure

The role of money in your relationships with other people can add strength and meaning to your financial structure, or, over time, create weaknesses that may undermine the stability of your plan. Your work in Level Four will help you create a new awareness of the role money plays in some of your relationships. This work will be the bricks and mortar of your edifice.

MONEY AND OTHERS

No financial structure, no matter how sound, will leave us feeling secure unless we take into account our connections with others. Money enters in some way into nearly every relationship we have. We provide for those we care about; we create special experiences for family and friends; we assist those in need in our communities; we have professionals who provide us services of all kinds.

There is also the downside of involving money in our relationships. According to more than one study, for example, money is at the root of the majority of failed marriages in the United States. Often the love we feel (or want), the control we think we need, the power we imagine we have or should have, finds expression in our behavior with money. On any given day, we're surrounded by evidence of money's power to impact relationships.

Your spending plan will give you clues about your relationships in which money plays some role. Categories like Dependent Care,

Entertainment, and Gifts are good places to start. Make a list of your relationships in which there is a financial connection or where a financial issue plays a role.

NAME	CONNECTION TO MY FINANCIAL WORLD

As you think about these relationships, consider the ways that money is present in each of them. How does your use of money in the relationships contribute to the strength of your new financial structure? How might it eventually weaken your structure?

RELATIONSHIP	HOW IT STRENGTHENS MY FINANCIAL STRUCTURE	HOW IT MIGHT WEAKEN MY FINANCIAL STRUCTURE

As you consider the future, how will your relationships need to be addressed in terms of your financial life? This might include providing for a child's education, planning for the care of an aging parent, and your own retirement and estate planning. It could also include scaling back the financial support you give an adult child or choosing to spend less on gifts. The important thing to keep in mind is that you want the financial component of all your relationships to enhance the financial structure you're building.

FUTURE CONSIDERATIONS

WHAT NEEDS TO BE DONE

When you consider the list you just wrote, what feelings come
up for you?

Money is often drawn into especially sharp focus in the relationship of a couple. (If you're single, you shouldn't skip this section; the concepts and ideas it contains can be used in other kinds of relationships where money comes into play.) Today, the makeup of couples, and the ways in which they run their finances, are considerably more varied than they were a generation ago, when the model was a man who earned the money and paid the bills, and a woman who got a monthly allowance with which to manage the household. This has changed dramatically. Today, when I work with couples and their money, I see a wide range of expression in terms of money management. Some people combine their finances, pooling their money and sharing expenses equally. Others split expenses and keep their incomes separate. If expenses are split, many couples share fifty-fifty, while others are more comfortable with contributions that are proportionate to each partner's earnings.

Working on your financial structure in true partnership with your spouse or partner can be a very powerful experience. My clients Denise and Greg are a good example. When they first came to see me in 1993, their marriage, in their words, was "on the rocks." They had $20,000 in credit card debt and owed a large sum in back taxes. To save money, they had just moved from a nice apartment into a small, dingy one. Even more damaging to their relationship than their material circumstances, however, were the daily betrayals that had come to characterize their shared financial life.

Denise was completely out of touch with her own needs. She'd suppressed them because she felt there wasn't enough money to go around. Greg's attitude was that he'd try and meet his needs at any cost. He had taken to surreptitious bouts of spending, then suffered stress and anxiety about what would happen when Denise found out.

It was at this stage that they began to construct their financial hierarchy. They started tracking their income and expenses, stopped using credit cards, and explored their belief systems about money. The creation of a Monthly Spending Plan helped their communication, and this new openness allowed them to stop viewing one another as adversaries and begin working together.

Today, their marriage is characterized by mutual respect and love. There are no more "money secrets" between them. They've bought a house, and their total assets have reached an amount that was once unimaginable to either Greg or Denise. Not too long ago, Denise quit her job and started her own business. Now they come to see me once a year or so for what they call a "tune-up." During their last visit, Denise told me, "This work saved our marriage and changed the quality of our lives."

If you are like most people, there are probably some elements of the way you and your spouse or partner manage your financial life that work well, while others don't work as well (or at all) for one or both of you. The goal of your work in Level Four is to learn how to incorporate money into your relationships in a way that enhances, rather than decreases, your sense of partnership and belonging.

Does the way you and your spouse or partner handle money foster or hinder these feelings? How?

In an ideal world, how would you structure the financial life that you and your spouse or partner have together? What would serve you in a way that most enriches your relationship?

What's keeping you from having your shared financial life arranged in just such a way?

Another area in which money often plays a powerful role is our relationships with children. Some of our strongest feelings about money come up around the kids in our lives, whether they are our own offspring, grandchildren, nieces or nephews, or the children of a close friend. If we are parents, for example, we may work in a challenging career so that there will be money for college. Or we may choose to settle for a less expensive wardrobe so that our children will be better provided for. While there are many things we do for our children that are positive and life enhancing, there are other things that we do where our motivations are less clear.

We live in an era in which many adults are driven by the idea that the more we spend on our children the better off they will be. This may be doing a disservice to both our children and ourselves. Where children are concerned, we need to become as aware as possible of how our decisions to spend money are made.

TEACHING CHILDREN TO MAKE SOUND CHOICES

Just as they need to attend to a child's schooling, medical care, nutritional needs, and spiritual life, parents have a responsibility to teach children about money. You can model and share knowledge about healthy money behaviors with children of any age, but it's never too early to start teaching conscious choice making.

For example, let's imagine that it's fall, and you and your young son are going to the local pumpkin patch to buy a jack-o'-lantern. You've decided that you don't want to spend more than $10, but you haven't told your child that. When you get to the pumpkin patch, there are hundreds and hundreds of pumpkins to choose from, each with more personality than the next. Your child calls you over and announces with shining eyes, "I want these two big ones—one for each side of the front gate!"

When you explain that the two together cost more than you want to spend, your little one feels his choice was "wrong." He feels confused and—having no basis for making a choice—ends up offhandedly saying, "I don't really want a pumpkin today." (Or he throws a tantrum in hopes of wearing you down, so you end up spending twice as much as you wanted to just to end the embarrassing scene.)

Now imagine a different scenario. You have told your child before you leave home that he will get to spend $10 at the pumpkin patch. Explain that for $10, he can buy ten little pumpkins, three medium-sized pumpkins, or one very large pumpkin. Emphasize that within the parameters you have just told him about, he gets to choose. Now your child has some age-appropriate guidelines for making his choice. He ends up choosing ten small pumpkins, which he excitedly declares will go in each and every downstairs window for Halloween night. You have kept to your spending plan while at the same time giving your child an experience of conscious, responsible decision making, and of learning to deal with limits. Preparing children ahead of time for a shopping and/or buying excursion helps create an experience that is more positive and rewarding for both of you.

I remember once when I had my two young grandsons with me and needed to get my car washed. It was a simple Saturday chore, and I gave no thought, as we drove into the car wash, to whether or not we would be spending any money. We walked into the waiting room and found shelves (positioned, of course, at just the right height for small children) full of balls, games, stickers, stuffed animals—all kinds of tempting possibilities. At once, the three of us were in a maelstrom. They were dashing in two directions, grabbing things. I was dashing in every direction trying to put things back. I finally succeeded in calming them down. They finally succeeded in getting the toys they thought they wanted. But as I reviewed the incident later, I realized that none of us really enjoyed the experience.

It was no one's fault that this situation deteriorated, but it was my job either to have prepared my grandsons ahead of time or to think of ways of turning around the uncomfortable situation into which we had wandered. It's important that as adults we be aware of what drives our own financial decisions so that we can help our children develop a strong, healthy relationship with money. If this is started young, you can prepare your child for a lifetime of making strong decisions.

Describe a shopping experience you've had with a child or young person (or one that you, as a child, had with an adult).

How did the experience make you feel?

Level Four

As you think of your children growing and maturing, what skills and attitudes toward money would you like them to develop? What can you do to help them become conscious and effective with money?

Parents need to begin teaching children about decision making and values clarification long before a child has an idea of what money itself is all about. Providing children with the experience of making responsible choices and living within their means is one of the most loving things an adult can do. "Even people with great wealth need to recognize that their children must be equipped for the world in terms of money and work," says John L. Levy, a consultant on inherited wealth.

As children grow older, we are often tempted to continue stepping in financially whenever we're asked, bailing adult children out of financial difficulty and taking on other financial responsibilities that should be theirs. We do this sometimes even when it causes a financial hardship for us. Even at this age, however, our children can still learn from the values and behaviors modeled by the adults in their lives.

One of my clients, a wealthy single father, brought his daughter to see me right before she was to start college. He was going to handle all of his daughter's expenses while she was in school, but he wanted Chloe to have a spending plan. In her clothing category, Chloe penciled in a pair of $160 athletic shoes. Her father told her that he was comfortable spending up to $90 for athletic shoes. Chloe argued that she really needed the shoes. "I'm not saying you can't have the shoes," her father replied. "I'm just saying you'll need to pay for them yourself." When she was forced to evaluate how much the shoes really meant to her if it were her own money being spent, Chloe chose not to purchase the more expensive shoes. Giving children responsibility for spending decisions can often influence what they can and can't live without.

By helping your children see what's important to you regarding your own financial security, you are helping them develop their own financial independence. As you become more aware of your own behaviors with money, you'll begin to see opportunities for helping your children form strong values of their own in relation to money.

While different from your relationships with loved ones and friends, the relationships you form with your financial professionals are also an important part of your overall financial structure. Your team might include:

* A financial counselor to help you gain the awareness and skills you need to construct your new financial life

* A financial planner to help you select insurance and do retirement planning

* An attorney to help you with wills and estate planning

* An accountant to assist you with taxes and tax planning

We talked in Level Two about the importance of taking charge of your own financial planning process and learning as much as you can about how financial professionals work and what they can do for you. Now, as you consider your future needs, you'll want to put some of your education to work. Your ability to identify the professionals you may need to use, choose the ones who can work appropriately with you, and develop good working relationships with these individuals is a key to your financial success.

Remember Stacy, the realtor you met in Level Two? After she learned to stop spending and start saving, developed her spending plans, and educated herself in the basics of personal finance, she felt ready to expand her financial planning efforts and realized she needed a professional to help. Her first move was to make an appointment with the financial planner her father had always used. A partner in a large, prestigious firm, he was a reserved man who, Stacy told me, "didn't come out from behind his desk once in the entire time we met." He gave her a lot of information but didn't seem too interested in the questions Stacy had for him. "Even though his connection to my father made me want to use this man's firm," Stacy said, "I knew that the lack of personal contact and empathy just wouldn't work for me."

Stacy continued her search by talking with friends and business colleagues. She checked the credentials and professional affiliations of planners she interviewed and asked for references from each planner's clients. She continued her own financial education by attending free seminars offered by a local brokerage firm. Stacy's efforts paid off: she found someone whose style and values she felt matched her own.

Many people experience a reluctance when they think about consulting a financial professional. Your money history and the earlier exercises may already have put you in touch with some of the issues that underlie any hesitation you feel.

As you consider working with financial professionals, what thoughts, feelings, and ideas come up for you?

Rereading what you just wrote, make a list of the obstacles (attitudes, feelings, beliefs) that could hinder you from choosing and working successfully with one or more financial professionals. Opposite each entry on your list, write down one action step that can help you overcome your obstacle or objection.

OBSTACLE   ACTION STEP

As you move into your new financial structure and begin working more and more from within its walls, you will eventually need to speak with some type of financial professional. This may mean seeing a financial counselor to help you work on basics; hiring an attorney to draft a will or a financial planner to help you with retirement planning; or going to an accountant for tax advice. You will need to continue to be aware of the issues and obstacles that block your way and find ways of moving around them.

Remember, when you work with a financial counselor, financial planner, attorney, or accountant, you are not simply turning your financial life over to an alchemist who will mysteriously spin straw into gold. You are enlisting the help of a trained, certified professional whose job it is to help you achieve the goals you have set and whose progress you continue to monitor.

Reviewing What You've Learned in Level Four

As a result of the work you have done in these pages, you should be looking forward to moving into a whole new way of living your financial life. In Level Four, you have:

* Gained new awareness of the role of money in your relationships and explored how your use of money in relationships can strengthen or weaken your financial structure

* Examined the money issues that can arise in your relationship with a spouse or partner

* Learned about the importance of teaching children to make strong, conscious financial choices

* Gotten in touch with some of the obstacles that may, until now, have thwarted your efforts to choose and work with financial professionals

Now you are ready to complete your financial structure. Let's move on to Level Five.

Level 5

Your
Complete

Financial Structure

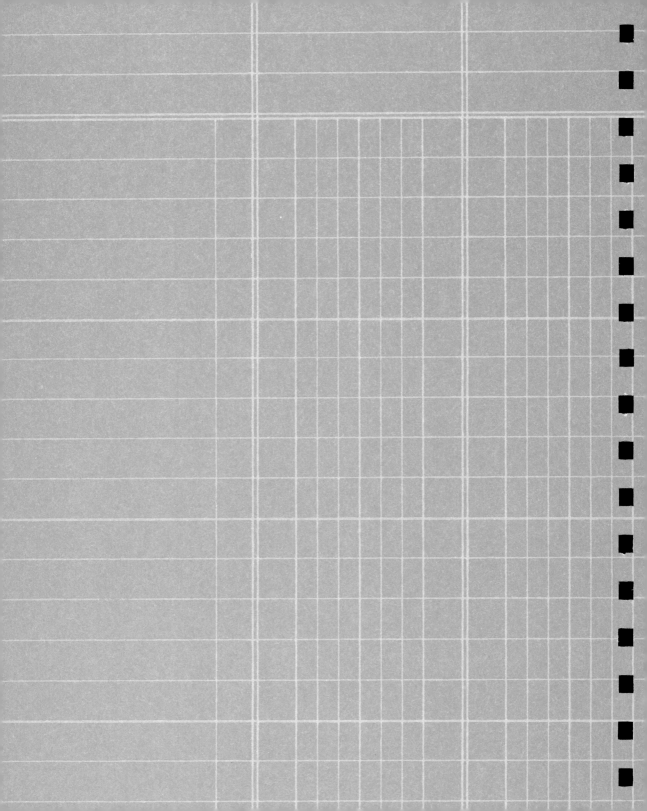

In the early years of this century, an explorer in Africa was observing a tribe of African hunters as they moved across the veld. Periodically, and for no apparent reason, they would stop for a time, and then continue on. After many days of observing this, he was allowed to approach the tribesmen. Through his interpreter, he asked their leader, "Why is it that you make these stops?" This ancient warrior looked out from beneath a proud and massive brow and answered the explorer in the same tone he might have used to instruct a small child: "Why," he said, "we are waiting for our souls to catch up." These pages have led you through both the pragmatic and the profound. As you reflect on what you learned as you worked through this journal, I'd like for you, too, to allow some time for your soul to catch up.

Pick a time and place where you will have as few distractions as possible. Surround yourself with whatever relaxes or comforts you. Pour yourself a cup of tea. Write whatever comes into your mind about your journey through these pages and your feelings about it.

Level Five

Level Five

When you first began this journal, what specific thoughts, emotions, or attitudes came up for you when you thought about planning your financial life? How have those changed?

BEFORE

AFTER

What do you feel you've accomplished from working through
these pages?

_____

_____

_____

_____

_____

_____

_____

_____

_____

_____

_____

_____

_____

_____

_____

_____

What words would you use to describe how you feel now about your financial life and the possibilities it holds?

Level Five

How do you think your life will change as a result of the work you've done in this book?

If I have done my job well, you are feeling a sense of exhilaration and hope—exhilaration at what you have already achieved and hope in the face of all that your newfound knowledge and inner strength make possible. This is the point at which you may be expecting me to encourage you on to still greater heights, and I'm not going to let you down. Because it's very important that you not stop here. Stay aware of the work you did in Level One, for these basics form the foundation of a sound, peaceful financial life. Remember that, as you learned in Level Two, savings and insurance are more than just financial tools. Along with education and action, meeting these important safety and security needs is the cornerstone for your financial peace of mind.

Continue to clarify your values around money, as you did in Level Three, and to be conscious of the part values play in your financial decisions. And as we discussed in Level Four, you will also lend strength to your overall financial structure by cultivating a greater consciousness of your money behaviors in relation to the world around you.

Take some time for reflection. When my husband's children were little, he would always have them sit with him after they had completed a project. Together they would admire the fruits of their labor. He wanted them to learn the importance of taking time to appreciate the act of creation. A necessary part of any project's completion is to simply stop and regard what you have done. The tasks for Level Five are fairly simple: Keep doing what you have been doing and adjust for change. From this point on, your sense of peace and purpose will continue to grow. But just as you would maintain a house or a garden, you will need to be mindful of the times when your financial structure needs some attention.

Take some time now to think about the maintenance your financial structure will need. Use the Personal Financial Hierarchy on the next page to write down your thoughts and ideas about what you'll need to be doing at each level. You can refer back to page 24 for guidance.

Your Personal Financial Hierarchy

Behaviors

What I want to do differently
from now on so that my financial
structure maintains its integrity

Benefits

What I will gain from my new financial
behaviors and the ways I maintain
my financial structure

PERIODIC
INSPECTION OF MY
OVERALL FINANCIAL
STRUCTURE

TOUCHING UP
THE BRICKS AND
MORTAR

CONTINUING
TO EXAMINE MY
FRAMEWORK

CHECKING MY
CORNERSTONES

MAINTAINING MY
FOUNDATION

As you carry on with your personal journey, remember that the soul searching you've done in these pages is not a one-time endeavor. There will be new events for which you will need to make adjustments. New people will enter your life, and others will leave it; a job will be lost or gained; you will grow older and your own needs will change. That invigorating ebb and flow that we call life will remind you again and again that the only constant we have in this world is change. Go back to the basics when you find yourself going in new directions. Remain aware of your needs and continue to assess your behaviors. Where something no longer works, try something different.

I would like to end this book the way I began it, with a hope that you will come away from these pages energized by new ideas, armed with a plan of action, and excited about what your future can hold. If you have done your work well and are willing to let your thoughts and feelings be your guide, you will begin to experience something deep and long lasting. It will spread from your finances to every other area of your life. You will feel the sense of calm that comes when you know that everything is being taken care of. At that point you will truly be able to tell yourself that you have planned your way to peace of mind.

Level Five

ACKNOWLEDGMENTS

It is hard to know where to start. So many people had a hand in bringing this project to fruition. First and foremost is my husband, John Glover. His keen mind, sound editorial judgment, and ever-present good humor were a joy throughout the writing of this book. His commitment to both the quality of the project and the sanity of the author never wavered, and his belief in both me and the work moved me profoundly.

Julie Wiles's commitment to the work was also an important part of what has ended up on the printed page. Her wordsmithing skills frequently helped me articulate my ideas in ways that surprised us both. David Shore of Marin Retirement Advisors in Larkspur, California, was an early believer in the importance of this book. I am deeply grateful for his friendship and for his willingness to share his knowledge with me at key points along the way.

I will likewise always be grateful to my two editors, without whom this book would not have come to be: to Allison Arieff, who had the vision to suggest this project to me in the first place, and then the fortitude to convince me—more than once—that I was up to the job; and to Leigh Anna Mendenhall, whose editorial savvy and passion for quality inform every aspect of the finished product. I value, more than I can say, the opportunity they gave me to write this book.

Others who helped bring this book to life are Carol Adrienne, Jeanne Alves, Marsha and Brian Burns, Denise Biernes, Carol Eejima, Candace Fuhrman, Bill Greene, Lynne and Michael Harding, Denise and Greg Hughes, Vince Kreizenbeck, Genevieve Leslie, John Levy, Kathleen Mitchell, Ed.D., Jerry Mapp, Stephanie Rice, Harriet Salinger, Barbara Stanny, Ted and Beth Streeter, and financial counselors Kathryn Amenta, Hudson Andrews, Maida Blythe, Lynne Boccignone, Kathleen Bowman, Danielle Bray, Yves Chinnapen, Lynda Ellis, David C. Ergo, Denise Hughes, Karen Eve LeCovin, Ph.D., Lee Loretz, Deborah Lusty, Deborah Miller, Lesley Scott, Richard Scott, Margaret Strang, Linda M. Tinkham, and Mikelann Valterra.

Special thanks are due to Nancy Christensen, Terri deLangis, Elizabeth Forrest, Dale Lancaster, Deborah Lusty, Christina Robinson, and JoAnn Towle, who tested many of the ideas and approaches you will find in this book. Their enthusiasm and insight contributed immeasurably to the work.

Finally, I want to thank my family, who gave me courage, love, and sustenance during the course of this project, and whose importance to this book and to my life cannot be overstated: Terri, Mark, Mathieu, and Nicholas deLangis; Tammie, Mike, and Jacqueline Mansuy; and Mike and Ian Glover.